A Trail Called Home

PAUL O'HARA

A Trail Called Home

Tree Stories from the Golden Horseshoe

DUNDURN
TORONTO

Cover image: Toronto skyline: shutterstock.com/Naniti; background texture: shutterstock.com/donatas1205; trail and trees: istock.com/MarinaMariya. Based on a concept by Paul O'Hara.
Printer: Friesens

Library and Archives Canada Cataloguing in Publication

Title: A trail called home : tree stories from the Golden Horseshoe / Paul O'Hara.
Names: O'Hara, Paul, author.
Description: Includes bibliographic references.
Identifiers: Canadiana (print) 20190060387 | Canadiana (ebook) 20190060417 | ISBN 9781459744790 (hardcover) | ISBN 9781459744806 (PDF) | ISBN 9781459744813 (EPUB)
Subjects: LCSH: Trees—Ontario—Golden Horseshoe. | LCSH: Human ecology—Ontario—Golden Horseshoe.
Classification: LCC QK203.O5 O33 2019 | DDC 582.1609713/5—dc23

1 2 3 4 5 23 22 21 20 19

Conseil des Arts du Canada | Canada Council for the Arts | Canada | ONTARIO ARTS COUNCIL CONSEIL DES ARTS DE L'ONTARIO an Ontario government agency un organisme du gouvernement de l'Ontario

We acknowledge the support of the **Canada Council for the Arts**, which last year invested $153 million to bring the arts to Canadians throughout the country, and the **Ontario Arts Council** for our publishing program. We also acknowledge the financial support of the Government of Ontario, through the **Ontario Book Publishing Tax Credit** and **Ontario Creates**, and the **Government of Canada**.

Nous remercions le **Conseil des arts du Canada** de son soutien. L'an dernier, le Conseil a investi 153 millions de dollars pour mettre de l'art dans la vie des Canadiennes et des Canadiens de tout le pays.

Printed and bound in Canada.

VISIT US AT

dundurn.com | @dundurnpress | dundurnpress | dundurnpress

Dundurn
3 Church Street, Suite 500
Toronto, Ontario, Canada
M5E 1M2

For Mom —

thanks for keeping me close to the trail.

One of the penalties of an ecological education is that one lives alone in a world of wounds. Much of the damage inflicted on land is quite invisible to laymen. An ecologist must either harden his shell and make believe that the consequences of science are none of his business, or he must be the doctor who sees the marks of death in a community that believes itself well and does not want to be told otherwise.

— Aldo Leopold, *A Sand County Almanac*

The problem comes when professionalism overwhelms intuitive vigour.

— John Ralston Saul, *The Unconscious Civilization*

Contents

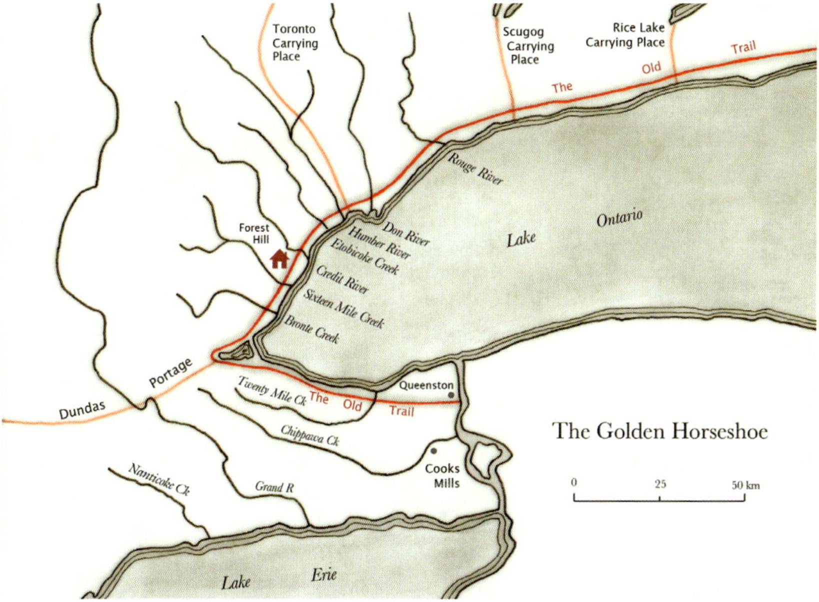
Toronto Carrying Place
Scugog Carrying Place
Rice Lake Carrying Place
The Old Trail
Rouge River
Lake Ontario
Forest Hill
Don River
Humber River
Etobicoke Creek
Credit River
Sixteen Mile Creek
Bronte Creek
Dundas Portage
Twenty Mile Ck
The Old Trail
Queenston
Chippawa Ck
Cooks Mills
Nanticoke Ck
Grand R
Lake Erie
The Golden Horseshoe
0
25
50 km

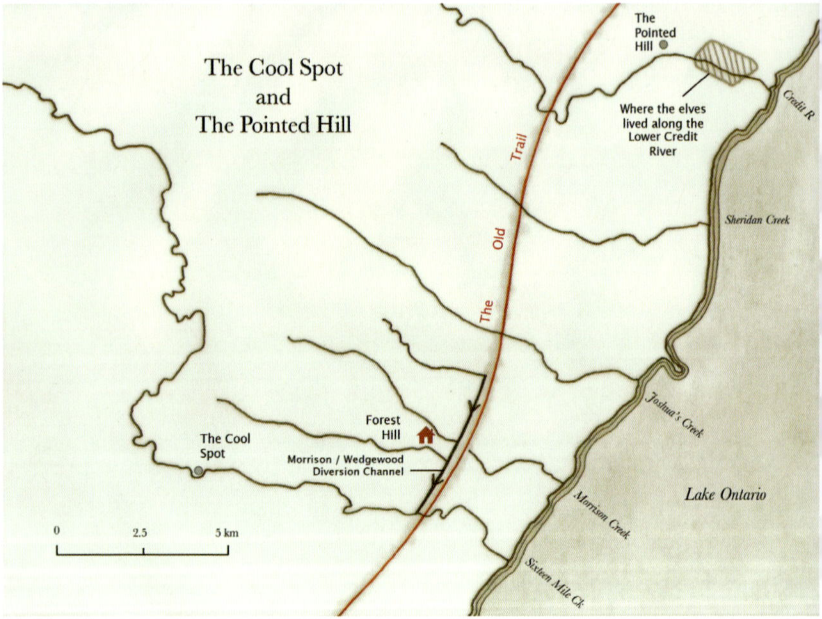

The Cool Spot
and
The Pointed Hill
The Pointed Hill
Where the elves lived along the Lower Credit River
Credit R
The Old Trail
Sheridan Creek
Joshua's Creek
Forest Hill
The Cool Spot
Morrison / Wedgewood Diversion Channel
Lake Ontario
Morrison Creek
Sixteen Mile Ck
0
2.5
5 km

My Forest Hill Neighbourhood
0
250
500 m
Upper Middle Rd
The Abandoned House
Trafalgar Road
White Oaks Blvd
Forest Hill
Lynnwood
Eton Place
Morrison Creek
Eighth Line
Iroquois Shore
Lake
The Bridge
Morrison / Wedgewood Diversion Channel
The field that went up in flames
Iroquois Shore Rd
McCraney Creek
McCraney St
The Jump
The Toboggan Hill
St Mike's School/Church
The Old Trail
Leighland Ave
Q E W
Sixth Line
Sewell Drive

Preface

I park my truck by the woods at the side of the road and get my field gear together. These days I dress in white painter pants and a white long-sleeved shirt so I can see the damned ticks. Ten, twenty years ago I could romp through the woods of the Golden Horseshoe without a care. Now, ticks are something you need to be wary of because one bite can make you sick or even kill you. I douse myself in DEET from the waist down to help keep the little low-lying buggers from latching on. From the waist up, to keep the 'skitters at bay, I spray on a homemade mixture of water, white vinegar, and essential oils.

I slip on my rubber boots and grab my orange safety vest to check the pockets are rightly packed for the botanical inventory I'm about to do: fully charged smartphone; GPS and extra batteries; clear 15-centimetre ruler; magnifying loupe; flagging tape; and a copy of *Newcomb's Wildflower Guide* in my chest pocket. In my small backpack, I keep water, a compass, Ziploc baggies for plant samples, and an extra reference book (it could be on sedges, grasses, asters, goldenrods, or ferns, depending upon the season).

Before starting out, I sprinkle a bit of tobacco by the edge of the forest. I learned about the offering of tobacco from my friends at the Mississauga of the New Credit First Nation. It feels good to do it, to pray to the land for a good outing and a safe return.

I start off down the skid trail into the fifty-acre forested tract in the Golden Horseshoe near Lake Erie. I'm usually a little nervous when I make those first steps into the woods, like there's a psychological residue of the city that I need to shake off before I can tune in to the beat

Preface

The flowers of an American chestnut, a tree species now listed as Endangered in Ontario.

of the land. But after an hour or so I start to shift down. My mind starts to calm. My heart rate slows. The mosquitoes, which buzz around and bite me for the first hour, have a harder time homing in on me as I start to blend into the green. I feel alert, yet at peace. At these times, I don't think of money, bills, relationships, time, or death. I just am, in the present, in the woods.

Most of us know that feeling when walking in a forest. It's that same feeling you can get while camping or being at a cottage — sipping a coffee by a lake at dawn or staring into a campfire at dusk. In the city, we can feel snatches of it in city parks or backyard gardens. The waving leaves. The birdsong. Eyes closed, feeling the sun on your face.

It's the natural frequency of humanity, of life. It's our natural idyll.

The First Nations of the Greater Golden Horseshoe — the Anishinaabeg, Huron-Wendat, and Haudenosaunee — built a whole philosophy, ceremony, culture, and attitude around that feeling of balance and communion with the land, in a time when all the land in the Golden Horseshoe was in a natural state, and they were immersed in it. Today, that communion with nature is increasingly hard to find.

In the late 1990s, I attended a talk by a prominent southern Ontario ecologist, Henry Kock. During the presentation, he showed a slide of a satellite map of the Greater Golden Horseshoe; he'd taken the photograph of his television while watching the weather report on the evening news. The image was dominated by the light green of agricultural fields and the grey of our cities and towns. The tiny, scattered blotches of dark green — indicating our remnant forests and wetlands — looked like an afterthought.

"Southern Ontario reads like a massive clear-cut," he said.

It felt like such a shocking thing to say, but it was true. We've pretty much taken it all. We've left very little forest standing — only about 15 percent across the Golden Horseshoe. And of that 15 percent, most of it is low-quality, isolated, and choked with invasive species.

The Golden Horseshoe lies in the Carolinian Zone of Ontario, the most biodiverse and threatened ecoregion in Canada. It has more species at risk than any other forest zone in the country. That loss of natural cover is the reason why I'm tromping through the woods today. My job is to find and document those species at risk, at least the ones that are plants.

On good days, I feel I'm helping the cause of conservation. Other days, I feel like I'm just documenting the decline as natural cover and species diversity in the Golden Horseshoe continues to dwindle.

After several hours in the woods I make my way back to my truck, tired and sweaty. Today was a good haul. I tallied a few dozen flowering dogwoods (an Endangered Species), a half dozen American chestnuts (another Endangered Species), and a couple of patches of a Provincially Rare sedge.

I change out of my field clothes, check them carefully for ticks, and start the drive back to my home in Hamilton. I feel relaxed, but also energized and refreshed. As I get closer to the city, I try to hold on to that woodsy calm, but it soon begins to fray.

What is it about cars that turn us all into assholes? Well, turn some of us into assholes, including me.

Driving on the country roads on the edges of the Golden Horseshoe can be relaxing and fun. I love the drive-by botany — studying the passing fields, hedgerows, roadside trees, and remnant forests. But once on the highway or in the city, there's no room for observing the land as the leisurely drive devolves into a high-speed go-kart race for stressed-out adults.

There's a smouldering tension that permeates the cities of the Golden Horseshoe. We're a civilization that moves too fast. We're an anxious civilization that sleeps less, dreams less. We're a civilization with conveniences that offer the promise of leisure, a leisure that, for most of us, never seems to come.

Of course, we're not going to go back to living in the woods, and I wouldn't want to. I enjoy the conveniences of modern life. But the pendulum has swung too far from our natural roots as we've become the only species on the planet that has effectively shunned its connection to the natural world.

Unconsciously, we know that we need to feed our senses with more nature and bring more of that woodsy calm into our lives. Why? Because our lives need magic. And magic is in the land. And the fact is, we're tied to that land, no matter how much we pretend we're not.

I've spent a lot of time thinking about how to persuade my fellow citizens to pay more attention to the land and the trees around them, and I kept on circling back to the same answer: through storytelling — the only way we humans have ever moved one another.

What follows are tales of the land that I've collected over twenty-five years of tree study, mixed with stories from my personal experience of growing up in the Golden Horseshoe.

Like most good stories, they are unremarkable and true.

1

On the Edges

"So, we going to The Cool Spot?"

That question was usually asked late on a Saturday just before we headed home, usually after a bunch of beers while we were partying either in the woods, in my townhouse garage (my mom used to tolerate us gathering there), or at the home of one of the guys whose parents happened to be away that weekend.

The weaving trunks of chinquapin oak on the south-facing slopes of the Sixteen Mile Creek in Oakville.

The Cool Spot was a Sunday retreat for our gang throughout our late teens and into our early twenties. Over five or six years we probably made the trek more than thirty times, in all seasons. We even camped out a couple of nights at our ramshackle forts.

Sunday morning came, calls were made. I'd collect my leftover beers in my pack and stand out on my driveway. A few minutes later I'd hear the lawnmower-like engine of my buddy Lee's old Mazda coming around the corner with Zeppelin, the Doors, or Crosby, Stills, Nash, and Young blaring from the tape deck. I'd jump in, and Lee would grab his pack of Du Maurier regulars, pop one in his mouth, and throw one my way. Car lighter popped, smokes lit, we were off to pick up the other guys. A stop at the Jug store for some dogs, buns, and more smokes and we'd be rolling up Trafalgar Road to Dundas Street.

As we turned off Dundas, we'd descend into the floodplain of the Sixteen Mile Creek at Lions Valley Park in Oakville, where we'd meet up with more of our gang. Fully assembled and looking like a pack of hooligans decked out in red-and-black-checkered lumber jackets, army pants, and all manner of bed-head, we'd start toward the unmarked trailhead, well away from the dozens of park patrons laid out on blankets, throwing Frisbees, and tending portable barbeques in the grassy parklands on the other side of the pedestrian bridge.

Then we'd take a path straight up the valley wall, a forty-five-degree incline. The red clay and shale crumbled underfoot as we'd wind our way through the stunted trees that clung to the slope. At the top, the land opened up into an old pasture bounded by forest. Here we'd stop and catch our breath before continuing north along the valley rim trail at the edge of the pasture. We'd walk single-file along the thin path, ducking under the low, heavy boughs of the trees perched on the valley edge. On the far side of the pasture, the trail entered open woodland and was blocked by a deep tributary valley of the Sixteen that we'd bypass by scaling down the valley, crossing the tributary, and climbing back up the other side. By the time we rejoined the valley rim trail, we'd have a good sweat going, and we'd skip along with greater ease.

The rising wind signalled our destination was close. A few more steps and the trail opened into a grassy flat. We'd reached The Cool Spot.

The slope, which dropped forty metres to the creek below, was populated by grasses and clutches of cedar. From the flat we had a wide view of the Sixteen valley, with its forested walls and shaggy floodplain willows. In the centre of the flat was our firepit, and within minutes we were seated on logs around a roaring fire, drinking beer and whittling weenie sticks.

I had my best fire-cooked dogs at The Cool Spot, when the sun was shining and a warm breeze blew through the valley. We never saw anyone out there besides a few folks on horseback from the farms along nearby Burnhamthorpe Road. The Cool Spot was our place — a place to relax and act like silly teenage boys.

After our campfire cookout, we'd roll rocks down the slope and listen for the splashes, then scale down the cliff and huddle in the cedar copses and smoke cigarettes and cook hash bottle tokes.

When the winds were high, we'd head for cover in the woods where we built a couple of half-assed forts that we'd throw together with hammers, nails, and handsaws — started but never finished. Here it was more of the same, sitting around a fire, cooking dogs, drinking beers, making up games, and taking the piss out of each other. We'd return home by late afternoon, exhausted, hungry for Sunday dinner, and a little more able to tolerate another week of high school.

The Cool Spot was our gathering place and, without ever saying it, we knew our pilgrimage to it was special. There was something that drew us teenagers there. I later learned that that pull was not unique to The Cool Spot. It exists throughout the entire Golden Horseshoe.

MEETING PLACE

It's been repeated many times for many years that the name *Toronto* comes from a First Nations word for "meeting place." Other interpretations have included "land of plenty" or "land of abundance." According to University of Toronto linguist John Steckley, the name *Toronto* actually originates from the Mohawk word *tkaronto*, which translates as "where there are trees in the water."

So, how does an error like this get repeated for so many years? It's because we want to believe it. It's stuck in the collective conscious of the citizenry because Toronto and the Golden Horseshoe feel like a "meeting place" and a "land of plenty."

The Dish With One Spoon treaty, negotiated three centuries ago between the Anishinaabeg and Haudenosaunee peoples of the Great Lakes/St. Lawrence Valley regions, actually does acknowledge the gathering and abundance qualities of this land. The treaty refers to the land as a place to be shared; a metaphorical "dish" from which all were free to hunt, gather, trap, and fish, while eating from a common "spoon." It is one of the oldest treaties in the New World, and unlike those negotiated between the First Nations and the colonial powers, it has never been broken.

The Niagara Peninsula and the north shore of Lake Erie were also known as a land of plenty. In *Early Narratives of the Northwest (1634–1699)*, French explorers Dollier and Galinée, while camped in Port Dover in 1669, marvelled at the richness of the land around them:

> I leave you to imagine whether we suffered in the midst of this abundance in the earthly Paradise of Canada; I call it so, because there is assuredly no more beautiful region in all of Canada. The woods are open, interspersed with beautiful meadows, watered by rivers and rivulets filled with fish and beaver, an abundance of fruits, and what is more important, so full of game that we saw there at one time more than a hundred roebucks in a single band, herds of fifty or sixty hinds, and bears fatter and of better flavor than the most savory pigs of France.

In 1822, the feisty Scot Robert Gourlay, in his *Statistical Account of Upper Canada*, also commented on the fullness of Niagara: "If there is one [spot] on earth intended for paradise more than another, it is this. In point of climate, soil, variety, beauty, grandeur, and every convenience, I do believe it is unrivaled…."

It's no wonder St. Catharines is called the Garden City and Niagara is Ontario's prime production area for tender fruits and wine.

The bounty of the Golden Horseshoe has been attracting human life since the retreat of the Wisconsin Ice Sheet more than twelve thousand years ago, when the earliest Indigenous People hunted caribou and other barren-ground mammals in the challenging tundra-like environment. As the climate warmed, the land was transformed from muskeg to boreal forest to broadleaf forest. The increased biodiversity spurred the development of more populous and socially complex Indigenous societies. Trade networks that ran from Lake Superior to the Gulf of Mexico and beyond were established. Sophisticated political systems blossomed. Subsistence based on hunting and collecting was replaced by sustainable horticulture. Camps became villages that were no less complex than their counterparts in medieval Europe.

Five hundred years ago, the Golden Horseshoe was largely the home of the people known to history as the Neutral Confederacy, a sophisticated and independent group of Iroquoian-speaking communities that lived in a "neutral" position between the Wendat (Huron) Confederacy to the north and the Haudenosaunee (Six Nations Iroquois) of what is now western New York

State. Tens of thousands strong, their villages ranged from Niagara north to Hamilton, as far west as London, and across much of the north shore of Lake Erie.

With the arrival of Europeans, and the economically disruptive trade goods that they brought with them, the First Nations of the Great Lakes basin found themselves pulled into longstanding European rivalries. As the demand for the pelts of fur-bearing mammals grew, the French and English pitted nation against nation in a proxy war for control of the fur trade. European writers of the day, who often emphasized Indigenous savagery for obvious political reasons, claimed that the Haudenosaunee slaughtered and dispersed the Neutrals around 1650. According to my friend Paul Racher, Principal at Archaeological Research Associates Limited, a more nuanced and likely reading of the historical record suggests that it is more probable that the Neutral Confederacy suffered severe population loss from imported European diseases such as smallpox, tuberculosis, cholera, and influenza. Those who survived were most likely adopted by the Seneca, the westernmost nation of the Haudenosaunee Confederacy, whose culture, lifestyle, and language was probably most similar to their own.

The Mississauga, a nation of strong, politically astute Anishinaabeg fur traders from the north shore of Lake Huron, moved into the Golden Horseshoe in the

1690s to fill the resulting void. The Mississauga enjoyed another century of hunting and gathering in this land before increased European settlement in the late 1700s pushed them into land surrenders they did not want and onto reserves where it was much more difficult to pursue their traditional lifestyle.

Since that time, millions have made the pilgrimage to the Golden Horseshoe, and today it is one of the most concentrated gatherings of humans on the planet. Almost nine million people — a quarter of the total Canadian population — call the Golden Horseshoe home, with another four million projected to move here over the next twenty-five years. More than one hundred different languages are spoken here and Toronto is recognized as the most culturally diverse city in the world.

But this gathering of life extends well beyond humans, to reptiles, amphibians, fish, birds, insects, and also to trees, as the Golden Horseshoe is the meeting place of three biomes.

Most places on earth belong to one specific biome, or large-scale plant community (e.g., rainforest, prairie, desert). In some places two biomes overlap at the edges — where temperate forest meets alpine forest or taiga meets tundra. But the Golden Horseshoe has the unique quality of being the meeting place of three rich and distinct biomes: boreal forest, deciduous forest, and prairie. It's the reason why there are more native trees here (over one hundred species, large and small) than anywhere else in Canada.

THE SOUTHERN EDGE OF THE NORTHERN WOODS

The boreal forest is Canada's largest biome. Sweeping in a broad band from Newfoundland to the Yukon, it functions as a huge carbon sink and has been referred to as "the lungs of North America," critical for mitigating climate change. In Ontario, the boreal forest takes up half the province from Sudbury north to Moosonee and west from Thunder Bay to Sandy Lake. But its influence extends well beyond that, into southern Ontario.

The trees of the boreal forest are common in Sault Ste. Marie and were some of the first trees I learned of while going to Sault College. Many of them are also prevalent in cottage country — in Muskoka, Haliburton, and Algonquin Park (an area of Ontario often called the Great Lakes–St. Lawrence forest: a transition area between the boreal forest biome of the north and the deciduous forest biome to the south). But in the Golden

Red pines at Lambton Park, Toronto.

Horseshoe, the trees of the boreal forest reach the southern limits of their range and their populations are few and far between, barely reaching below the climatic line of Highway 401 — the difference on some winter

(left) White cedars (with the shrub beaked hazel) grow on the steep slopes of The Cool Spot.
(right) Tamarack, white spruce, and white cedar grow in a swamp near Erin in Wellington County.

days between snow in Guelph and rain in Hamilton, black ice in Brampton and puddles in Pickering.

In fact, the trees of the boreal forest that persist in the Golden Horseshoe are remnants from the retreat of the Wisconsin Ice Sheet, and therefore, in the much warmer climate of today, can live only in our coldest corners: north- and east-facing slopes; windswept ridges; kettle bogs; and conifer swamps. These tree species include evergreens such as black spruce, white spruce, white cedar, and balsam fir; the deciduous conifer tamarack; the northern Great Lakes conifer red pine; and hardy deciduous trees such as white birch, trembling aspen, and many of our shrub willows.

THE NORTHERN EDGE OF THE SOUTHERN WOODS

Most of the trees in the deciduous forest biome of the eastern United States range throughout Appalachia, reaching their southern limits in east Texas, Louisiana, and northern Florida. What's incredible is how many of these same trees reach the extreme northern limit of their range in the Golden Horseshoe.

The Head of the Lake at Hamilton — the westernmost point of Lake Ontario — is a natural pivot point between the Great Northern Woods and the Great Southern Woods. Red mulberry and pignut hickory

A pawpaw grove in St. Catharines. **(inset)** Pawpaw fruits.

reach around the Head of the Lake and into the rocky slopes and ravines below Waterdown. Chinquapin oak, American chestnut, and flowering dogwood make it as far north as Oakville, while sassafras stretches along the lake plain into the Beach neighbourhood of Toronto. Dundas is the northern terminus of tuliptree; black gum reaches, just barely, into the southern corner of Hamilton Region; while cherry birch, shellbark hickory, pawpaw, hoptree, and cucumber magnolia don't make it north of Niagara Region.

Most of these southern trees are uncommon in the Golden Horseshoe while others are downright scarce. They are exotic arboreal jewels to be discovered among more common forest trees like sugar maple, red oak, and white pine. For Golden Horseshoe tree aficionados like me, these trees are a fascination and a delight to see in their native habitats; places like Bronte Creek Provincial Park in Oakville, the Dundas Valley in Hamilton, Short Hills Provincial Park in Niagara, and Backus Woods in Norfolk County.

THE EASTERN EDGE OF THE GREAT PLAINS

In the 1970s, tree freaks puzzled over the small, deeply scalloped leaves of an oak that grows on the well-drained soils of the Norfolk Sand Plain from Hamilton to Long Point on Lake Erie. Some thought the trees were scarlet oak, and early floras listed scarlet oak as native to southern Ontario. It took until the early 1980s for researchers to identify the mystery tree not as scarlet oak, but as Hill's oak, a tree more commonly found in the

Midwest prairie states of Minnesota, Wisconsin, Iowa, Illinois, Indiana, and Michigan.

In pre-settlement times (before European settlement), Hill's oak was found on the tallgrass prairies and oak savannahs around the Head of the Lake. Today, it persists in remnant woodlands, hedgerows, and rural roadsides around Hamilton, Cambridge, Brantford, Tillsonburg, Port Dover, Simcoe, and Delhi. These are the only places in southern Ontario where it grows (although Hill's oak was first discovered in northwestern Ontario on the border with Minnesota).

Bur oak, hackberry, and rock elm are trees of the Midwest that are also at the east end of their ranges in the Golden Horseshoe. Like Hill's oak, bur oak is another prairie and savannah oak from the Great Plains. It's our hardiest oak, just as happy growing on the clay plains of the Golden Horseshoe as it is on northern prairies near Winnipeg. Hackberry doubles between the rocky slopes of the Niagara Escarpment and near floodplain habitats (especially of the Grand and Thames Rivers), while rock elm persists in small stands on the limestone bedrock of the Flamborough Plain north of Hamilton, on the gravelly soils of north Halton Region, and on a few hills north of the Greater Toronto Area (GTA).

(right) A pair of cucumber magnolias in a private forest in Fonthill, Niagara Region.

(left) Sassafras on the north shore of Cootes Paradise near Bull's Point, Hamilton Region.
(right) A young pin oak grows in a roadside ditch in fall, near Ridgeway, Niagara Region.

THE EDGE EFFECT

The southern edge of the boreal forest, the northern edge of the deciduous forest, and the eastern edge of the Great Plains meet in the Golden Horseshoe. The overlapping edges of these three biomes create ecotones: areas with greater biodiversity than can be found in the individual biomes. This heightened species richness or synergy is commonly referred to in biology as the "edge effect."

I can't help but think that the cultural diversity of the Golden Horseshoe is at least partly a consequence of this heightened natural diversity or edge effect — why more native trees grow in the Golden Horseshoe than anywhere else in Canada, and why more people have met here than anywhere else in the country, almost anywhere else in the world. Anyone who studies the natural areas of the Golden Horseshoe or walks its streets can feel the deep sense of gathering that permeates the land.

When I returned from college with my newfound education about trees, The Cool Spot was the first place I experienced that edge effect and sense of gathering in nature. It was the first place I noticed how the west-east course of the creek created cool, north-facing slopes populated by hemlock, white cedar, and white birch, and hot, south-facing slopes populated by oak, hickory, maple, and white pine. It was the first place I saw chinquapin oak (the stunted trees on the forty-five-degree incline), the first place I saw an extreme-southern stand of red pine (at The Cool Spot itself), and the first place I got to know the plants of the tallgrass prairie (no Hill's oak, but lots of prairie-affinity species on the hot valley rims — species like big bluestem, blueberries, woodland sunflower, New Jersey tea, bastard toadflax, silver-rod, and Seneca snakeroot).

The hike to The Cool Spot became a benchmark for my budding botany skills, a place that I have returned to many times since my first tree identification course twenty-five years ago, and a place that I will return to for the rest of my life.

But my love of the land around me really started in my early childhood.

2

Out the Door

I grew up on a street called Forest Hill, just off White Oaks Boulevard in the town of Oakville, which lies roughly halfway between Toronto and Hamilton. We (Mom, Dad, brother Patrick, and sister Deirdre) moved there in 1976 when I was six years old. Forest Hill was nothing like the upscale neighbourhood of Forest Hill in nearby Toronto; rather, it's in a typical middle-class neighbourhood built in the 1960s, back when they still made houses that didn't all look the same. Ours had white vinyl siding, dark green shutters and shingles, and a matching green front door.

Forest Hill was on what was then the northern edge of Oakville (today, the northern edge has pushed north of Dundas Street some three kilometres away). The population of Oakville has tripled since I was a kid and the rural lands between Milton and Oakville continue to fill up with houses. Back in the 1970s, to the north there were only a few apartment buildings (still there today) and a young Sheridan College — but beyond that there was nothing but farms, fields, and forest. To the west across Trafalgar Road was McCraney Creek. To the east was Morrison Creek. To the south was Trafalgar Road hill, which overlooked the Q.E.W. highway, distant Old Oakville, and Lake Ontario.

The woods along McCraney Creek were my first arboreal stomping grounds. It was the perfect creek for me, my brother, and our friends on Forest Hill. It was child-size, half a metre at its deepest and three or four metres at its widest, with lots of pebbled shallows that could be forded with minimal soakers. My friends and I would explore up and down its banks and marvel at the flitting water striders, darting minnows, and lumbering crayfish. We'd flip over shale looking for salamanders,

The Forest Hill Gang. Left to right: Me, my buddy Lee, my brother Patrick, and my buddy Bar, on Forest Hill, 1982.

chase garter snakes from their sunny retreats, and capture toads in cupped hands. We'd wade through the wildflowers in spring, kick through the leaves in fall, and crack through the ice in winter. As the sun went down, my dad would walk up the hill in our backyard and blast a two-finger whistle across Trafalgar Road, and we'd run home.

By our preteens, our adventures in the natural world continued all over Oakville. My friends and I would just get on our bikes and go. We biked the forest trails of Morrison Creek and then down to the lake to swim off of the Oakville pier or skip rocks on the cobble beaches. We'd bike to the big creek, Sixteen Mile — really a river, named for its distance from the Head of the Lake or Hamilton Harbour. Here, we'd strap on chest waders and snag salmon with treble hooks and cook hotdogs over creekside campfires. The deep valley walls of clay and Queenston shale gave the Sixteen a wild and faraway feel. The Sixteen Mile Creek was the first place I saw larger wildlife like deer and fox, water snakes and great blue herons, the first place I heard hooting great horned owls and yipping coyotes.

When my friends got their driver's licences, we began exploring the land in borrowed family cars in ever expanding circles. Almost always, we'd head northwest to the conservation areas along the Niagara Escarpment. We hiked the rocky trails at Crawford Lake and Rattlesnake Point, played shinny on the frozen swamps at Burns Conservation Area, biked the backwoods trails at Hilton Falls, and rappelled into the caves at Mount Nemo.

Sometimes we just went on "boonie cruises" after school. Once clear of the town limits, we'd float along the rural roads — 4th Line, 6th Line, Lower Base Line, Tremaine Road, Burnhamthorpe Road, Britannia Road — and stare out at the passing fields, hedgerows, and forests. At railway crossings we'd coax the driver (like he needed it) to gun it and we'd all wave our hands like we were on a roller coaster. I think we sometimes actually got air.

We continued to explore our natural surroundings into our late teens and even into our early twenties. That was when we stopped visiting the last fort at The Cool Spot and life became more complicated by the drudgeries of "higher learning" and "career development." But I never felt like I was wasting time in the woods. It was like I was preparing for something. What that was, I didn't know then.

In high school, I wasn't sure what I wanted to do as a career. Does any kid know? I think most of those who did were pressured into something by a helicopter parent. Mine were too busy with their own lives. Mom was working two jobs to pay the bills, and Dad, who I saw on the weekends, was remarried, working on a second family, and busy with his own job. At the time, I never considered that I could have a career that allowed me to hang out in the woods. No teacher or guidance counsellor ever talked about trees and forests or careers in biology or ecology in high school, especially at St. Ignatius of Loyola, where math and science (physics and chemistry) were preached as the Son and Holy Ghost.

I worked a slew of summer and part-time jobs throughout high school — chasing buggies and stocking shelves at a grocery store, pushing around a mower on a grass maintenance crew, making portable construction heaters on an assembly line, filling orders for bacon keepers and lettuce crispers at a Tupperware outlet — and knew I didn't want to do any of those jobs as a career. About the closest I got to working in the woods at the time was a summer tree-planting job in Armstrong, a logging town about three hours north of Thunder Bay.

I was seventeen, the kid on an all-male crew of early twentysomethings. The first night in Armstrong we stayed in a motel and, while curled up in my sleeping bag on the floor, I was awoken at 2:00 a.m. by raucous laughter. Pretending to be asleep, I cracked one eye open to see some of the guys gathered around the edges of the bed taking hauls off a tall metal tank. When one of them took a hit, their eyes would roll back and they'd fall back on the bed in a fit of laughter and euphoria. Apparently, some of the guys had the bright idea to steal a tank of nitrous oxide, or laughing gas, from a business down the street and bring it to the motel room for some head-spinning fun. This was the first clue that I had hitched my wagon to a carload of clowns.

The next day we set up camp in the woods near our planting site and set to work stuffing sad-looking spruce and pine seedlings into the hard, rocky soils. After a week of planting, an RCMP officer rolled into camp to quiz some of the guys about the missing tank. Turns out the officer had no proof, but ended up bluffing the crew leader into spilling the beans and wieners about the theft of the tank and its disposal in the lake next to our campsite. That was it for my tree-planting adventure. I wanted out. Luckily, one of the smarter guys — not involved in the theft and who had his own wheels — had had enough of the circus, too, and I successfully convinced him to take me with him on the twenty-hour drive back home. I got paid nothing for the work and swore off ever going tree planting again.

Upon graduation from high school, I went to Wilfrid Laurier University for math, and I hated it from the beginning. Admittedly, I had trouble keeping up with the advanced calculus and algebra, and found learning in the big lecture halls too impersonal. But most of all, I was swept away by the thrill of independent living and spent more time drinking beer with friends down the street at the University of Waterloo's Bombshelter Pub and kicking a hacky sack around the grounds of the University Centre than I ever did opening any books at WLU.

So, after a couple of semesters I called it quits and landed a student job with the City of Waterloo cutting grass and tending annual beds in Waterloo Park while I figured out my next move. What was I going to do with my life?

During the summer of 1993, I flew to Sault Ste. Marie to visit some university friends. The airport there is out in the woods on the edge of town and, having brought my bike, I cycled into town upon landing. Rolling down the rural road I was immediately captivated by the sights, smells, and sounds — the buzzing insects and croaking ravens, the rich wetlands and clear creeks, the scent of pine and spruce, the hint of cool in the August air, and most prominently, the granite hills of the Canadian Shield curling up into the Algoma Highlands and beyond. I fell in love with "the Soo" that weekend and started in the Forestry program at Sault College in January of 1994.

The courses in the first semester of the Forestry program were interesting enough — Forest Biology, Forest Mapping, and Forest Mensuration. But in Forestry 101, Introduction to Natural Resources, I was miffed when I was graded on how well I sharpened my axe. You got extra marks if you had the creativity to carve your initials into it, ensuring you were always chopping down trees with *your* axe and not someone else's. The disparity between the advanced math courses at Laurier and the axe sharpening was enough for me to switch into the more challenging Environmental Engineering program. But during that semester in Forestry, I took the one course that would change the direction of my life: Dendrology, the study and identification of trees.

In the course, we learned about the native trees of Ontario and their habitats. We learned how to tell the difference between the smooth leaf margins of sugar maple versus the toothed margins of red maple; the pointed lobes of red oak versus the rounded lobes of bur oak; the whorled needles of black spruce and flat needles of balsam fir; the simple, spade-shaped leaves of basswood versus the compound leaves of white ash; the smooth bark of beech versus the flaky bark of black cherry. We learned common shrubs and even a few wildflowers.

We walked through the bush across the road to field test our classroom lessons. We went on bus trips into the Algoma Highlands, strapped on snowshoes and learned how to identify trees in their winter condition using silhouettes, bud characters, and twig arrangements. We studied the forest zones of Canada — the Maritime, the boreal forest of the north, the aspen parklands of the prairies, the montane of central B.C., the coastal forests of B.C., and the Great Lakes-St. Lawrence forest of Quebec and central Ontario. When we discussed the deciduous forest region or Carolinian Zone of southwestern Ontario, my ears perked up.

An ancient pathway through an oak woodland on the Bronte Creek in Oakville. I believe this path is a short remnant of The Old Trail that once wound around the entire Golden Horseshoe.

Up until then, I didn't think where I grew up was that special. It wasn't like any of the nature shows I watched on TV as a kid. No lions chasing gazelles on the savannah. No monkeys swinging from jungle trees. No bighorn sheep hopping around snow-capped mountains. Besides the Escarpment, some hills, and forested ravines, my home was a flat land full of cars, roads, houses, buildings, and humans — lots of humans.

But in that class I learned that the Deciduous Forest Region covered much of the eastern United

States through Appalachia and reached into southwestern Ontario and the Golden Horseshoe where I grew up. I remember being dumbfounded. Some seventy-plus tree species grew there? The richest forests in Canada? The same forests that I played in as a kid? It was a revelation.

A door opened.

On school breaks I returned to my childhood home of Oakville with a new sense of adventure. Clutching the eighth edition of R.C. Hosie's *Native Trees of Canada*, I went back to all my old haunts in the woods. Back to the McCraney and Morrison Creeks, back to the Sixteen Mile and Bronte Creeks, back to Mount Nemo, Rattlesnake Point, and Hilton Falls. As a kid, I passed the trees in these forests without a care. Now, they all had names and I was determined to get to know them.

I learned the trees of the Great Lakes–St. Lawrence Forest Region that occurred in both Sault Ste. Marie and Oakville, such as white pine, hemlock, red oak, bur oak, and sugar maple. And I learned the trees of the Deciduous Forest Region — trees that were found in Oakville but not in the northern woods of Sault Ste. Marie — such as white oak, black oak, bitternut hickory, shagbark hickory, black walnut, and sassafras.

Back at Sault College, I took the year two dendrology course. I was no longer in the Forestry program, so this was a course I wasn't registered for, but the instructor allowed me to sit in on the class because I was so stoked to learn more about trees and how to identify them.

As I spent more time in the forest, I got to know the personalities and preferences of the different trees — how the beech shies away from the sun and the black oak seeks it out; how the ironwood sits below the canopy while the white pine pushes above it; how the beech, sugar maple, hemlock, and yellow birch gather in groups; how the red oak, white oak, shagbark hickory, and white pine do the same; how the basswood, white ash, bitternut hickory, and black cherry mingle among them all.

Wherever I went, I looked at trees: walking, biking, on city buses and GO trains, in the mixed forests of the Soo when I was at school and in the deciduous forests of Oakville when I came home to visit. I began keeping field books, scrawling notes about the places I hiked, the habitats, and the notable trees I saw along the way. I dug out the old Minolta SLR my dad had given me as a kid and began photographing my botanical explorations.

Forest outings with my old gang of friends in Oakville changed, as I was now off in the bush staring at the ground or up into the canopy. That was when the joking began as one of them would call out, "Hey Paul!? Didja find dickweed!?"

But I couldn't help myself; the trees and other plants had all their own personalities and I wanted to meet them all.

I graduated from Sault College with a diploma in Environmental Engineering and went on to Fleming College in Lindsay where I earned a diploma in Ecosystem Management. Over the next ten years I got jobs in horticulture, forestry, botany, and ecological restoration, all working in the Greater Golden Horseshoe. I worked at the City of Waterloo, Town of Oakville, Lower Thames Valley Conservation Authority, Toronto Region Conservation Authority, Catholic Cemeteries of Hamilton, and in the science department at Royal Botanical Gardens in Burlington. I began guiding tree hikes and teaching public programs on tree identification.

When I wasn't at work, I was learning on my own, deep in the fields, forests, and wetlands of the Golden Horseshoe, all the while working my way through shrubs and wildflowers and more difficult plant families like ferns, grasses, and sedges. My home of southern Ontario began to feel larger as I learned to recognize and name more of the plants in the wilds all around me.

In 2004, after ten years of plant study, I started my own business designing and building native plant gardens and naturalization projects, and working as a consulting field botanist. These experiences have taken me to hundreds of natural habitats across the Golden Horseshoe and beyond. It's been twenty-five years since that first dendrology course at Sault College and today trees remain my primary study and fascination.

Trees define so much of Canadian life, but so many people, particularly in the Golden Horseshoe, don't know much about them. Granted, it's harder here; there are more trees that are native to the Golden Horseshoe than anywhere else in Canada.

Trees are the great storytellers of the landscape, looking glasses into the past. Trees speak of biology, ecology, and geology. Trees speak of aspect, prevailing winds, soil moisture, and fertility. They speak of natural history, First Nations history, and colonial history. Trees also speak of power and spirit.

Through a greater understanding of trees, we can tap into that power and spirit and become more rooted to the land beneath our feet, and our place in it.

3

In the Street

Trafalgar Road has a hill that runs up what used to be the shoreline of glacial Lake Iroquois, and that hill was a constant fixture of my childhood. On clear summer days my friends and I would stand on the edge, peer across the lake, and say we could see Buffalo — the place where fires were always in the news and Commander Tom lived. This was before cable TV; at the time, one of the few channels was Buffalo 29, so we had a lot of Buffalo news and loved its kids' program, *The Commander Tom Show*.

On the edge of the hill at White Oaks Boulevard are the grounds of Oakville Town Hall, where we played soccer and baseball in the summer. On the west side, where Trafalgar Road meets McCraney Road, the hill was our toboggan run, and we spent many winter weekends racing down it on plastic saucers, Krazy Karpets, and old-school wooden toboggans. We'd even steal a few runs on the way to school by squatting on our Adidas bags, those bicoloured imitation leather track bags that all the kids had back then. By Christmas, all the knobs on the bottom had popped off and we'd be asking for new track bags.

We had a love-hate relationship with the hill. When the sun was long, we'd run down the sidewalk on Trafalgar Road and hop the shadows of the passing cars, losing ourselves in laughter. On our bikes we could achieve the craziest tire-wobbling speeds, slamming on our brakes before we hit the lights at Leighland Avenue at the bottom. It was always fun going down, but the hikes back up the hill after long days of play were gruelling and often we had to get off our one-gear bikes and push.

When I look at the hill at Trafalgar Road today, I think about those old times, and wonder about times

Road Between Kingston and York, Upper Canada, by James Pattison Cockburn (ca. 1830). This is the Old Danforth Road, built through the pre-settlement forests from Scarborough to the mouth of the Trent River.

even older, when my Forest Hill neighbourhood was exactly that: a wooded promontory above the lake plain. I imagine what it would have been like to stand at the top, peer through the trees, and catch a glimpse of the forest canopy below and the great lake in the distance. I think of McCraney and Morrison Creeks before they were cut in half by the Morrison Wedgewood Diversion Channel, and what they might have looked like in their natural states.

But more than anything, when I look at Trafalgar Road hill, I wonder about The Old Trail, which ran along the bottom of it. As Hazel C. Mathews wrote in *Oakville and the Sixteen* (1953),

> About a mile farther inland was an earlier road which had been used for ages by the Indians. It was a link in the long trail leading from Quebec on the St. Lawrence River to New Orleans at the mouth of the Mississippi River. In the vicinity of Oakville the trail ran at the foot of the low ridge a mile from the lake. Known locally as the Red Hill, this ridge is the shore cliff of Lake Ontario's predecessor known to geologists as Lake Iroquois. The land south of the ridge was gravelly, level, and dry, and

> whenever practical the Indians made use of this prehistoric shore line.

Trafalgar Road hill was called Red Hill back then because of the red clays and shale that the hill is made of. The hill bends around the entire Golden Horseshoe. They say the trail that ran below it may be around ten thousand years old, dating back to the retreat of the last ice age when the Golden Horseshoe was muskeg and Indigenous Peoples hunted caribou and shrinking numbers of mastodons and woolly mammoths. Around that same time, the lake plain was underwater, the St. Lawrence River was plugged, and Lake Ontario drained into the Hudson Valley through New York State.

At Trafalgar Road, The Old Trail would have run somewhere near where Oakville Place Mall is, probably along Leighland Avenue and the aptly named Iroquois Shore Road.

Going west, the trail roughly followed the North Service Road through Oakville and along Harvester and Plains Roads through Burlington. In Hamilton, the trail continued along York Boulevard to King Street, Highway 8, and Regional Road 81 to Queenston, better known today as the Niagara Wine Route.

Going east, the ancient trail bent north near the Ford Drive/Q.E.W. bottleneck, loosely following

Dundas Street through Mississauga and west Toronto. Through the heart of Hogtown, the trail followed Davenport Road, eventually meeting the lake's shore in Scarborough. Farther east, the trail paralleled Highway 401 through Durham and Northumberland Regions, maybe along the 401 itself, the "gravelly, level, and dry" ridge now highway roadbed.

I was born near The Old Trail where it crossed Etobicoke Creek north of Etobicoke General Hospital and have lived beside it for most of my life: seventeen years on Trafalgar Road hill, six months in Beamsville on the shore bench, two winters in Toronto at Gerrard Street and Woodbine Avenue, one year in Oakville at Sixth Line and the Q.E.W., and six years in Hamilton's Corktown neighbourhood. The first house I bought was a few steps from The Old Trail where it ran near Dundurn Castle in Hamilton.

Is there something that draws me to these ancient travelling routes? Something in the landscape that is imprinted on us in childhood that lays down imaginary breadcrumbs we feel compelled to follow? *Stay close to the trail and you will find your way home.*

The trail below Forest Hill may have been the oldest, but there were many others that First Nations used for travelling throughout the Golden Horseshoe and beyond. The Toronto Carrying Place trail was the Highway

400 of yesteryear, a portage route that ran from the mouth of the Humber River at Lake Ontario north to the Oak Ridges Moraine, where the headwaters of the Humber kiss the headwaters of the Holland River. But the Toronto Carrying Place trail was just one of several routes from the Golden Horseshoe to the lake and river systems of the Canadian Shield. The Scugog Carrying Place trail went from Oshawa to Lake Scugog; the Rice Lake Carrying Place trail went from Port Hope to the west end of Rice Lake; and a diagonal trail ran below the Niagara Escarpment through Milton, Glen Williams, Palgrave, and Beeton to Kempenfelt Bay at Barrie.

In pre-colonial times, First Nations trails were found along almost every major waterway and dry ridge in the Golden Horseshoe, and some of today's roads still follow these ancient routes. In Toronto, parts of Riverside Drive, Weston Road, and Islington Avenue follow the Toronto Carrying Place trail. East of Orangeville, Hockley Road follows a former trail along the Nottawasaga River. In Port Credit, lower Mississauga Road traces a First Nations path that ran along the west side of the Credit River. And Lakeshore Road echoes an old trail that followed the Lake Ontario shore.

In Burlington, Snake Road, named for its side-winding nature, was a trail from the mouth of Grindstone Creek to the top of the Niagara Escarpment.

A neighbourhood built in an old-growth forest: Red oak, beech, and white pine in Roseland in Burlington.

The hill at John Street in downtown Hamilton follows another old Escarpment ascent, and Mohawk Road on Hamilton Mountain skirts a shallow ridge where a First Nations path joined Ancaster with Queenston.

The Dundas Portage was an ancient route west from Dundas to Brantford and beyond. This route was part of the Detroit Path through southwestern

Ontario, crossing the Grand River and following parts of Highway 53 through Burford to the Thames River, along the Thames to Detroit, connecting to the Sauk Trail through southern Michigan and the Midwest and, finally, to the trail systems of the Great River (as Hazel C. Mathews mentioned, it's said to have gone to New Orleans at the mouth of the Mississippi).

First Nations trails also ran along the Grand River connecting Lake Erie in the south to headwater trail systems, which led to Georgian Bay or Lake Huron.

In Niagara, a large network of trails connected the Falls and Chippawa, Fort Erie, and Niagara-on-the-Lake, the Short Hills, Point Abino, and Sugar Loaf Hill at Port Colborne. From the present-day hamlet of Cooks Mills, trails spun off in all directions, and streets like Chippawa Road, Chippawa Creek Road, Lyons Creek Road, Doan's Ridge Road, Beaverdams Road, River Road, the Niagara Parkway, and Ridge Road follow these old routes.

First Nations trails like the one that ran below Trafalgar Road hill were the first "streets" of the Golden Horseshoe. They connected settlements and sacred sites, hunting camps and fishing grounds. They led to freshwater springs and gathering areas for berries, nuts, roots, bark, herbs, mushrooms, medicines, and teas, and provided construction materials for wigwams, longhouses, palisades, and canoes. These trails were the trading highways to other nations in southern Ontario and across North America. Young, fit First Nations runners carried messages to neighbouring bands along these routes and could travel the one hundred kilometres from Niagara to Toronto in a day.

The winding First Nations forest trail stands in sharp contrast to the static street grids of today. The meditations of the First Nations runners wouldn't be possible with today's frenzy of cars and trucks; the host of grazing game and hunting predators have been replaced by midnight raccoon raids and the daytime skittering of squirrels; the chorus of various forest songbirds have been succeeded by the chirping of house sparrows and starlings; and well-worn paths then fringed with ferns, trilliums, bloodroot, baneberries, foamflower, and phlox are now hardened into asphalt, concrete curbing, and a monotony of Kentucky bluegrass.

What was once the great trailside window that peered into the heart of the richest forests in Canada has been largely supplanted with a whole new suite of trees, most of them immigrants like many of us.

THE NEW ARRIVALS

Old World settlers brought Old World trees with them, and today they dominate most of the streets of the Golden Horseshoe. Norway maple is far and away the most commonly planted tree in our streets. Native not only to Norway, but to much of Europe, more than a dozen varieties are offered in local nurseries, including the 'Harlequin,' with its variegated leaves; the 'Globosum,' with a compact, globular form; and the popular 'Crimson King,' the maple that displays red/maroon leaves throughout the growing season.

Other commonly planted Euro-exotics in our streets include little-leaf linden, with its spade-shaped leaves and strap-like flowers; horse-chestnut, with its showy spring flowers, spiky nuts, and tired crinkly foliage in late summer; and English oak, most often seen in its fastigiate form — columnar wisps stuck in tight urban spaces.

Most of the evergreen trees in our streets are also from Europe. The two most common Old World pines in the Golden Horseshoe are Scots and Austrian. Scots pine's contorted orange-coloured crowns are a semi-frequent sight in older residential neighbourhoods, while Austrian pine is a denizen of townhouse and apartment complexes where children quickly learn not to play around their long, pointed needles. Norway spruce is another commonly planted Old World conifer of our streets. It has banana-sized cones and drooping secondary branches that remind me of a 1970s Ozzy Osbourne, arms outstretched in a tasselled leather jacket.

Some of the Old World trees are drifters, planted with good intention years ago; their seeds travel around reproducing in the cracks, crannies, and corners of our cities. They lean on walls, loiter on corners, climb on fences, hitch on roadsides, hide in hedges, and are abundant in urban centres like Hamilton and Toronto.

Native to China, tree-of-heaven is the ultimate vagabond. With thick branches and compound leaves that suggest sumac, tree-of-heaven will eke out a living on the poorest of urban soils, heaving asphalt wherever it goes. White mulberry is another drifter from the Far East, often seen as the umbrella-shaped standard in suburban front yards. Urban birds eat the berries and poop them out all over the city, spreading the tree far and wide. Russian olive and Siberian elm are other champion drifters that are quickly colonizing our highways and byways.

And the exotic street tree list goes on and on: ginkgoes and magnolias, copper beeches and callery pears, weeping birches and mountain ashes, Sargent cherries and Siberian crabapples, sycamore maples and Japanese yews, Turkish hazel and Japanese maples, English elms and weeping willows. And I haven't even mentioned the glut of smaller non-native trees and shrubs planted in formal beds and beside foundations: lilacs, privets, junipers, boxwoods, hollies, hibiscus, hydrangeas, forsythias, and burning bushes.

Norway maple in flower over downtown Hamilton.

Most of the exotic trees in the streets of the Golden Horseshoe have their redeeming values. Some were planted for sentimental reasons as a reminder of homelands left, some for their showy flowers or unique forms, and others for their tolerance to urban growing conditions. Some, like the over-planted Norway maple, might have some utility in our bleakest urban centres, well away from natural habitats where it can displace native trees. Others, like tree-of-heaven, Siberian elm, and white mulberry shouldn't be planted at all because of their ability to spread quickly throughout our cities.

The main problem with exotic trees is that our native insects — the basis of the food chain — haven't forged an enduring relationship with them like they have with our native trees.

Doug Tallamy, entomologist at the University of Delaware, laid out this argument in his landmark 2007 book *Bringing Nature Home*:

> When a plant is transported to an area of the world that contains plants, animals, and diseases with which it has never before interacted, the co-evolutionary constraints that kept it in check at home are gone, as are the ecological links that made that plant a contributing member of its ecosystem. In an ecological and evolutionary sense, the alien plant's new neighbors won't know what to make of it and, in most cases, will exclude it from their biological interactions. The plant will occupy space and use resources (light, water, and soil nutrients) that would otherwise have been

> available for a native plant, but it will not pass the energy it harnesses from the sun up the food chain.

When we plant our streets and our gardens with non-native trees, shrubs, and perennials, we deprive our native insects, as they do not recognize these plants as food. When we deprive our native insects, we deprive every other animal up the food chain, including our native birds and mammals. According to Tallamy, "A plant that has fed nothing has not done its job."

Likewise, the exotic trees in our streets say nothing about the land in the Golden Horseshoe, as their stories are rooted elsewhere. So I pass them by.

When I walk the streets of the Golden Horseshoe, I look for the native trees that tell the stories of this land and the spirit of our pathways of old.

ORIGINAL BEAUTIES

A few years ago, my mom gave me some old photos from our time on Forest Hill. One of them shows my sister and me playing in our backyard in the winter of 1977. I'm standing on the deck and Deirdre is tobogganing on the small hill that separated our yard from the roar of traffic on Trafalgar Road. In the background across Trafalgar Road are the McCraney Creek woods,

(above) My sister and I tobogganing in our backyard on Forest Hill in 1977. In the background, across Trafalgar Road, are the McCraney Creek woods.

(left) What's left of the woods today. These are the original trees that remain on Trafalgar Road after the forest was destroyed.

the first forest we played in as kids. These woods were part of a large block of tableland forest that extended west to the McCraney Creek valley. In the late 1970s, the buildings on nearby Marlborough Court were built and much of the forest was removed. Today, all that remains are a couple dozen native trees — white pine, sugar maple, red oak, basswood, and shagbark hickory — growing in the turf beside the sidewalk on Trafalgar Road. Some of these trees may be nearly 150 years old. They are original trees.

Original trees are relics of the Golden Horseshoe's natural habitats, now stranded amid the urban and suburban neighbourhoods that have been built up around them over the last two hundred years. They're the oldest living things in our streets and, in many Golden Horseshoe neighbourhoods, the last voices of our local natural heritage.

Original trees aren't lined up like soldiers as are the planted, exotic trees in our streets. They stand a little offbeat, singly and in clusters, on boulevards, highway edges, and property boundaries, butted up against fences or too close to sidewalks. They are often large trees, towering over houses and hanging over streets.

Some were saved by tree-loving citizens in decades past as our cities and towns grew in a wave over remnant forests. Others were saved by the luck of the draw, being

An original white pine in Roseland in Burlington.

far enough away from road and building footprints not to be a bother. Still others were transplanted from back-forty forests through government tree-planting programs in the late 1800s that paid farmers a quarter for each tree that survived three years.

Naturally, the original trees in our streets are the same species found in the forests of the Golden Horseshoe: sugar maple, red maple, beech, white pine, red oak, white oak, bur oak, black oak, shagbark hickory, basswood, black cherry, and white ash, among others.

I look for original trees wherever I travel in the Golden Horseshoe. I admire these old friends in the streets around my home, and look for new friends when I travel through unfamiliar neighbourhoods.

Almost every neighbourhood in the Golden Horseshoe has original trees, and some neighbourhoods have many. Everyone knows the feeling of being in these neighbourhoods — the dappled shade, the coolness of the air, the rustle of leaves in the high canopy, the birdsong. Streets that slow the heart, charge the senses, and invite exploration.

When I graduated from college, I spent two unemployed winters living in Toronto with my dad and his wife, Donna, at their home in the Beach. I was broke and riddled with school debt. When I wasn't mailing CVs and cold-calling environmental consulting firms, I was exploring the original tree neighbourhoods of Hogtown.

Every morning before going to work, Donna would leave me two TTC tokens and my dad would leave me a couple of bucks for coffee. Armed with a map and an oversized Tim Hortons travel mug, I was off for the entire day along the Bloor-Danforth subway line in the Beach, Leaside, the Annex, Swansea, High Park, and Parkdale; communities whose vertical space is decorated by big, beautiful, red, white, and black oaks. Navigating the icy sidewalks under their snow-laden boughs eased the stress and worry of debt and unemployment.

When I finally landed a job at Royal Botanical Gardens in Hamilton as a student gardener, I spent the weekends biking through the original-tree neighbourhoods of Burlington and Oakville: the white pine and oak on the sandy hills along North Shore Boulevard through Aldershot; the beech, sugar maple, white pine, red oak, white oak, and white ash in Roseland; the oak, pine, maple, and black walnut along Lakeshore Boulevard; and the hundreds of original oaks, maples, and white pines that crowd the bungalows and backsplits of east Oakville.

An original white oak on South Street in Dundas.

An original black maple on King Street in east Hamilton.

An old original bur oak on Kipling Avenue in Etobicoke.

The drooping vase-shaped form of a mature white elm at the back of Morden Park in Oakville.

After I bought my first car, I began exploring the edges and the spaces in between: the oaks and white pines in the neighbourhoods of Mineola, Port Credit, and Lorne Park; the bur oaks, basswoods, and black maples on the streets of Guelph; the sugar maples of Kitchener-Waterloo; the bur oaks of Cambridge; and the black oaks of Brantford.

In more recent years, I've been exploring the streets on the ends of the Horseshoe: the few original trees in the streets of Durham Region (Pickering, Ajax, and Oshawa) and the incredible original-tree streets of Niagara Region (Fonthill, St. Catharines, Thorold, Welland, Niagara Falls, and Niagara-on-the-Lake), where, if you look closely, you can find rare originals such as pignut hickory, pin oak, flowering dogwood, sycamore, sassafras, and tuliptree gracing their boulevards.

And since moving to the Head of the Lake twenty years ago, I've scoured the streets of The Hammer. The closest originals to my home are three white oaks in Dundurn Park at the corner of Rolph Gate and York Boulevard and a black oak at the base of Locke Street at Tecumseh. Moving farther out, there are the black maples on George Street, the bitternut hickory on Margaret Street, the shagbark hickory on Ravenscliffe Avenue, the white oak on Burris Street, and the red oak pillar on West Avenue South in the Stinson neighbourhood. There are the old original oaks in Westdale Village, downtown Ancaster, and the Driving Park in Dundas, as well as dozens of original sugar maples, bur oaks, and shagbark hickories that adorn the neighbourhoods on the Mountain brow.

I know my home by the original trees in my neighbourhood. They are living road signs and natural landmarks. They are powerful reminders that we haven't been here long, that this is a recently altered landscape. Original trees strengthen my connection to the land like no human construction can do, and it feels good to put a hand to their bark or give them a nod as I pass them by.

But when I travel our streets, I also see how quickly we are losing them.

Every year hundreds of original trees are removed from the streets of the Golden Horseshoe due to old age and the stresses of street life. We lose many healthy original trees to road expansion and the whims of indiscriminate homeowners and contractors during home renovation projects. Some Golden Horseshoe neighbourhoods have lost, or are on the brink of losing, all their original trees, and with them, the last signs of their local natural heritage.

Some original trees have weathered one hundred or even two hundred winters, and a few even more than that. When an original tree is lost, we lose the ecosystem

Original sassafras trees on Mountain Road in Niagara Falls.

services it provided for local wildlife. We also lose the stories of the land that it carries in its boughs: trees that remember Hurricane Hazel, the Great Depression, the rise of industry, and the birth of Canada. Trees that were saplings during a time of shipbuilders, blacksmiths, icehouses, gristmills, and the old general store. Trees whose lineage stretches deep into the prehistory of this land, when First Nations Peoples were the sole stewards and the streets of the Golden Horseshoe were pathways through the primeval forest.

In an age when our streets are quickly becoming anonymous and bereft of regional personality — the same old big-box stores, shopping plazas, car dealerships, coffee shops, and variety stores — original trees stand as rich reminders of the character of this land.

Fortunately, some good things are happening to stem these losses. Dozens of local conservation groups are celebrating their urban forests with tree education/planting programs, and citizens are demanding stronger tree bylaws to protect heritage trees. City parks and forestry departments are planting more native trees, conventional nurseries are offering more native tree choices, and landscapers and their clients are beginning to ask for them by name.

The bad news is that most nurseries don't track the provenance of the trees they sell — meaning they don't know where the seed that grew the tree is from. You could be buying a white pine grown from seed cones collected in Vermont, or a sugar maple propagated from whirlybirds harvested from a forest in Illinois. A red oak grown from a Pennsylvania seed source may be unable to take the cold of an Oshawa winter. A red oak grown from a Sudbury seed source may buckle under the heat and humidity of a St. Catharines summer. This is one of the reasons many of our street plantings fail in the long run: their genetics are not suitable for this land. They may be native species, but the seed source is key.

Furthermore, if you buy a cultivar (cultivated variety) of a native tree (e.g., 'Brandywine' red maple, 'Redmond' basswood, or 'Shubert' chokecherry), you

Original red oaks at Queen's Park, Toronto.

are planting a tree clone that was propagated asexually through tissue culture, so all the trees are genetically identical. Since genetic diversity is the key to healthy ecosystems, cultivars do little to help boost the genetic diversity of our urban ecosystems.

This is where seeds from our original trees can help. Original trees know how to live here — in our climate, with our moisture cycles, our day length, our hot, humid summers, and damp, slushy winters. They interact with our soil food web and are familiar to our mammals, amphibians, reptiles, birds, and insects.

For every original tree in our streets today there were many others that succumbed long ago to life in the

White pine and sugar maple on a roadside in Oshawa.

street. The original trees in our streets today are survivors who have proved their hardiness to the stresses of street life — the car exhaust, smog, soil compaction, road salt, twenty-four-hour lighting, and biweekly bumps from lawnmowers and weed-whackers.

After two hundred years, the results from this serendipitous genetic selection experiment are in: the original trees that stand in our streets are the hardiest of stock.

But most original trees in our streets haven't produced a single seedling in decades. Every year their seeds cover our streets, sidewalks, and lawns only to be raked into piles, pawed into paper bags, and left on boulevards for disposal. Yet each seed carries a blueprint to grow another giant to decorate our streets and carry on the stories of this land.

We could be collecting the maple keys, ash samaras, oak acorns, hickory nuts, and pine cones and sowing them on our properties, or growing a few potted trees to share with a neighbour, school, or place of worship. Citizens who live in strong original tree neighbourhoods with robust gene pools could be sharing seeds with those who live in neighbourhoods lacking original trees. Residents of the Beach could plant a few acorns, those in Roseland could sow some beech nuts, those on Hamilton Mountain could gather some maple keys, and those citizens who today live on Forest Hill could be collecting seeds from those originals on Trafalgar Road — a great hobby for the retiring baby boomer.

By gathering the seeds of our original trees and growing them in our modern pathways, we can bolster the health of our urban ecosystems and preserve the spirit of the primeval forest and its ancient pathways in the streets of the Golden Horseshoe.

Road
A L G A R
HIGHWAYS
RAILWAYS

4

In the Field

On the opposite page is a 1954 aerial photo of the lands around Forest Hill — before the houses there were built, before Sheridan College, before Oakville Place Mall, when the Q.E.W. was a lazy four-lane highway for Fairlanes, Hornets, and Skylarks. The large block of forest in the centre is the McCraney Creek woods. The snaking wooded creek to the north is the Morrison. Before the Morrison Wedgewood Diversion Channel was put in, McCraney Creek was a tributary of the Morrison and they met at the bottom of the Red Hill, or Trafalgar Road hill. The lands had been cleared and farmed for a century by this time and any trace of The Old Trail below the hill was long gone.

By the time my family moved to the area in 1976, the built areas of Oakville had reached just north of Forest Hill. The farm fields beyond became rich sources of exploration for our gang.

When we were first allowed off Forest Hill on our own, my friends and I played in a field at the end of our street, just across Lynwood Drive. We'd wade through the grass in high summer and giggle as the grasshoppers bounced off our skinny legs. We'd marvel at the mantids and walking sticks, throw potato bugs into spider webs, sear crickets with magnifying glasses, and smack sticks against the "smoke bomb" fungi and watch them puff out their spores.

One hot summer day the field went up in flames and the fire trucks came. It was a big event and the whole street came out to watch. My buddy Lee swears to this day that the grass fire was caused by his magnifying glass, which he had lost in the field in the days before the fire.

When we were allowed to roam farther, we'd walk to the end of White Oaks Boulevard (back when it dead ended at the apartment buildings), cross the steel barrier, and explore the pastures and hedgerows that bordered Morrison Creek. Here, we'd get chased by farm dogs and hightail it to the safety of nearby hedgerows, jailing ourselves in their nest of thorny branches.

The fields and thickets north of Sheridan College were another one of our pre-teen playgrounds. We'd snoop around the abandoned farmhouses and race our BMXs through the motocross trails along Upper Middle Road, back then a two-lane, rolling country road.

During the summer of 1982 our gang hung around an abandoned farmhouse in the centre of a patch of scraggly, young woods north of Sheridan College. The house was torn apart and its contents were strewn about the site — piles of wood, bricks, old windows, and rusty appliances. Here, we'd carry on like curious boys, climbing on the piles, fishing through the junk and, of course, throwing rocks at the windows.

The last day we ever went to the house we saw two dogs tied up among the debris. They were barking like crazy and we kept our distance. All of a sudden, a man in a trench coat with a camera popped out from behind one of the piles and began snapping photos. We all screamed and I ran east towards Trafalgar Road while the rest of the guys ran south towards Sheridan College. I bee-lined it down the narrow path through the thicket for half a kilometre and didn't look back until I emerged huffing and puffing on the edge of Trafalgar Road. It was only then that I realized I was alone.

I met up with the guys a couple hours later and we exchanged our excited stories. Trench Coat Man chased them through the thicket all the way to Sheridan College. That was when they ran up against the ten-foot-high chain-link fence at the athletic track and had to climb, the last one of them getting their foot above the top before Trench Coat Man reached the fence and finally gave up his chase.

Our forays into the fields on that northern edge of Oakville were reserved for weekends and summer holidays, but walking through fields was also an everyday adventure. Our walk to St. Michael's Elementary School took us along a well-worn path through the meadows along Sewell Drive. Depending on the time of year, the path had standing water and mud holes we'd jump over, or icy bits we'd slide across, and we often showed up at school with soakers, mud-splattered shoes, or, in winter, ice-crusted pant legs that rubbed together like sandpaper and echoed down the halls.

In the spring there were calling frogs, meadow nesting birds, and tent caterpillar nests we'd poke sticks into. In the fall we'd have crabapple fights when the thorny trees would fruit. Sewell Drive was the battle line and we'd launch our ammo from either side of the street, the cars passing underneath the arcing fruits.

A large thicket of these thorny trees grew beyond the grassy path north of Sewell Drive. This same thicket extended to the back of St. Mike's, where the grade eights would smoke cigarettes and neck, and farther west to the back of Montclair Elementary School that was the site of "The Jump" — an earthen BMX ramp built into the edge of the thicket.

The Jump was where all the BMXers would gather to get air and show off tricks like "one footers," "cross-ups," "rhinos," and "tabletops." Some of the older kids were pretty rad and would get so much air they would crash into the bushes when they landed.

It wasn't long before my friends and I lost our playgrounds in the field. By the mid-1980s, the meadow across Lynnwood Drive was paved into a parking lot for the Trafalgar Professional Centre, the thicket along McCraney Road was bulldozed for town homes, and the grassy path along Sewell Drive was scrubbed into a clean concrete sidewalk lined with fresh sod. White Oaks Boulevard punched through the dead-end steel barrier, bulldozing the meadows and thickets on the west side of Morrison Creek, and Upper Middle Road was graded into a four-lane cross-town artery. Hundreds of houses were built on either side of Upper Middle Road to become the neighbourhoods of College Park, River Oaks, and Iroquois Ridge North. Today, the edge of Oakville has pushed into the fields north of Dundas Street more than two kilometres from Forest Hill, its sights now set on Burnhamthorpe Road.

Almost every adult who grew up in the Golden Horseshoe can describe a similar tale of losing their childhood playgrounds as suburban, retail, and industrial development rolled out across the fields.

In recent decades, the cities and towns of Durham Region (Oshawa, Pickering, Ajax, and Whitby) and the communities north of Toronto (Markham, Thornhill, Newmarket, Richmond Hill, Vaughan, and Woodbridge) have ballooned into the surrounding region. In a generation, Mississauga and Brampton have gobbled up much of rural Peel Region. In Guelph, Kitchener-Waterloo, and Cambridge, developers continue to find space among the moraines and drumlins for more housing and industry, even under the pressures of a fragile water supply. On Hamilton Mountain, bulldozers push south into lands curiously not part of

A cornfield on the edge of Brampton.

the Greenbelt, and the blossoming economy of Niagara Region continues to threaten their rural lands.

Land disturbance has always been a part of the ecology of the Golden Horseshoe — a fundamental element of the life cycle of the earth itself — but it's changed exponentially over the last 250 years. In pre-settlement times, disturbance on the land came from a greater balance of natural and human causes.

FIRE

When the first explorers began trickling into the Golden Horseshoe in the 1600s, First Nations populations numbered in the tens of thousands — not enough to alter the land on a scale comparable to the disturbance we see today (some nine million people now inhabit the area). Still, they had a great effect on the land around them.

The Anishinaabeg moved on a seasonal rotation through the landscape, building small camps and temporary shelters (wigwams) along creeks and rivers. The people of the Neutral and Haudenosaunee nations built villages with several to dozens of longhouses next to their agricultural fields, and when the nutrients in their fields began to be depleted, they picked up and moved their villages elsewhere.

First Nations people used fire to shape the land for their benefit: to clear the land for settlement and agriculture, to control pest populations, stimulate grazing areas to attract game, and to boost nut production. These fires created vast prairies and savannahs of oak, hickory, and pine, and the nuts (oak acorns, hickory nuts, and hazelnuts) were a key source of nutrition for First Nations. When settlement began, these open habitats were noted by early explorers and pioneers.

In the 1790s, Lady Elizabeth Simcoe described the prairies at the Head of the Lake around present-day Dundurn Castle as "quite like a park, with large oak trees dispersed, but no underwood." Poet R.K. Kernighan described downtown Hamilton in 1875 as a "monotony of Indian Grass." In 1836, author and naturalist Catharine Parr Traill described the "plains" around Peterborough as "[forming] a beautiful natural park, finely diversified with hill and dale…." Botanist John Goldie's field notes through downtown Toronto in 1819 also described "plains," where the only trees that grew were a "stunted growth of gnarled oaks." And in 1824, Colonel Edward Talbot remarked on the prairies of Brant County: "From the Indian Settlement on the River Ouse [Grand River], to the village of Burford, a distance of nearly 13 miles, there is not an acre of woodland to be seen."

Staghorn sumac flowers on a Burlington roadside.

Already clear of timber thanks to First Nations clearance by fire, these grasslands became sites of natural choice for many early settlements. Peterborough, Toronto, Port Credit, Burlington, Hamilton, Ancaster,

Dundas, Brantford, Paris, Simcoe, Niagara-on-the-Lake, and Niagara Falls were all built, at least in part, on tall-grass prairie and savannah habitats.

Today, the prairie heritage of the Golden Horseshoe has been nearly obliterated from the landscape, reduced to a few scraps along roadsides, railway corridors, hydro rights-of-way, and in protected areas like High Park and Lambton Park in Toronto, Bronte Creek Provincial Park in Oakville, the Niagara Parkway, and along the Grand River through Brant County.

HEAVY WEATHER

Severe weather has also played a part in disturbing the land in the Golden Horseshoe, as the area lies at the northern edge of an active weather region where tornadoes, downbursts, severe lightning storms, and even hurricanes can occur.

Of course, the most well-known modern weather event of the Golden Horseshoe was Hurricane Hazel, which effectively flushed the communities along the lower Humber out into Lake Ontario in October 1954. But many other fierce weather events have been recorded over the years.

In 1884, for example, a tornado half a kilometre wide levelled churches, barns, and stables in Elora. And the year 1829 brought several violent storms that wrought destruction and death on the towns of Guelph, Galt, and Niagara-on-the-Lake.

Hurricane Road in Fonthill got its name from a violent storm that hit the area in 1792. According to the *Jubilee History of Thorold* (1898), the storm levelled "all the houses in its path, but at the same time uprooting the trees, thus effectually clearing the woods. A road was afterwards built through this storm-swept region from Fonthill to Port Robinson, and was appropriately named 'Hurricane Road.'"

And then there was "The Big Wind." An early settler counted the rings on a young pine growing up in the destruction zone and figured the storm came through in 1755. This date was confirmed by a First Nations elder who returned home from hunting that year to find his whole family had disappeared. The storm is said to have left a hole a mile wide, and its path of destruction stretched for forty kilometres across Halton Region. An F5 tornado (with wind speeds exceeding four hundred kilometres per hour) has never been recorded in Ontario. But the Big Wind, as it was called by First Nations at the time, might have been such a tornado.

The course of the Big Wind can be tracked through the 1806 land surveys of Samuel Wilmot as it cut southeast through Halton and Peel Regions. Wilmot described thousands of acres in the destruction zone as "old windfall," noting only the occasional poplar or pine. The Big Wind twisted its way through what is now downtown Milton, Drumquin, Erin Mills, and Erindale, entering Lake Ontario at Port Credit. It was said that in the storm's aftermath you could stand at Milton and marvel at the jumble of "huge trees rotting under mounds of earth" walled in by the standing forest on either side.

PIGEON POWER

The passenger pigeon was another force of land alteration in the Golden Horseshoe. It is estimated that one quarter of all the birds in eastern North America at one time were passenger pigeons, and the Golden Horseshoe was an active nesting area.

Flocks would return to the same sites year after year and large breeding grounds were witnessed along the Sixteen Mile Creek, at Pine Orchard east of Aurora, and along the Mimico Creek in Etobicoke (First Nations called Mimico "The Home of the Wild Pigeon").

Ernest Thompson Seton described the spring migration of passenger pigeons through the Don Valley in *Life-Histories of Northern Animals* (1909):

> I shall never forget the last great horde that passed over, it was in 1876 about April

> 20th. An army of pigeons flew overheard due north. The flocks seemed only about twenty deep but extending east and west as far as could be seen fading into a smoky line on each horizon. There must have been hundreds of thousands in that flock and it was succeeded by others of similar extent every half-hour for most of the day. I saw it all from my bedroom window and I must sorrowfully add that it was the last of the great flocks, that according to record, ever came over Toronto.

The huge flocks looked like long "passenger" trains, and millions of birds would descend to the forest to roost with a deafening noise, piling one on top of another, the branches breaking under their weight. Flocks could cover hundreds of acres, and their accumulated dung would pile up, killing the trees and the understory vegetation below. Early settlers would follow the pigeons to their roosts looking for an easy meal, and flocks were so dense that one gunshot could kill dozens of birds.

The rampant hunting didn't help, but the primary reason the passenger pigeon went extinct was because of the logging of the old-growth forest of eastern

North America; these birds depended on the beech, maple, and elm fruits for survival.

The last large flocks flew over the Golden Horseshoe in the 1870s and the last breeding pairs in Halton Region were recorded near Campbellville in 1886. Martha, the last known living passenger pigeon, died at the Cincinnati Zoo in 1914.

A giant funnel cloud, a forest canopy filled with birds, a line of fire sweeping through a prairie … there's a romantic quality to disturbances of the past. These disturbances, while destructive, also breathed life and diversity into the landscape, and most importantly, left the land intact and able to regenerate.

Since European settlement, land disturbance in the Golden Horseshoe arose more and more from human sources — a recent history and well-known refrain. From the forest clearing, agriculture, and construction of our early roads and communities in the 1800s powered by horse, ox, water, steam, and elbow grease, disturbance has evolved into what it is today: a diesel-fueled dagger with excavators, trenchers, tillers, tractors, backhoes, bobcats, and bulldozers. These machines can farm thousands of acres in a matter of days, or construct condo towers, industrial buildings, and hundreds of houses in just a few months.

High wind events like tornadoes and downbursts continue to be part of the disturbance cycle in southern Ontario, and dozens are reported every year. But the passenger pigeons and the traditional settlements of First Nations are gone, and besides a few controlled burns to manage today's prairie remnants, the fires are gone, too.

When the land is disturbed, and then allowed to regenerate, it undergoes succession. Meadows turn into thickets. Thickets turn into young forests. The trees of the field are responsible for making that transition from field to forest happen.

The trees of the field are sun-lovers that seek out openings on the land. In pre-settlement times, the trees of the field worked in the natural forest gaps, in the blowdowns, in the forests scarred by the pigeon roosts, on the charred prairies and savannahs, and in the abandoned settlements and agricultural fields of the First Nations. Today, the trees of the field work on whatever lands are still available for regeneration: vacant lots, roadsides, fallow fields, hedgerows, forest openings and edges, and in the grassy playgrounds built for today's kids who live on the margins of our ever-expanding cities and towns. Here's how the transformation from field to forest happens.

An early successional forest of red ash, white elm, gray dogwood, and American plum near Jarvis, Haldimand County.

The first plants to colonize disturbed land in the Golden Horseshoe are not trees, but annuals, biennials, and weak perennials like pigweed, goosefoot, sow thistle, mustard, fleabane, foxtail, crabgrass, barnyard grass, witchgrass, and ragweed. Over time, the meadow becomes more diverse as longer-lived perennials move in, such as native aster, goldenrod, common milkweed, black-eyed Susan, wild bergamot, and evening primrose, as well as exotic perennials like Queen Anne's lace, dandelion, teasel, ox-eye daisy, St. John's wort, chicory, cow vetch, clover, buttercup, and thistle.

Where native prairie grasses (switchgrass, Indian grass, little bluestem, big bluestem, and Canada wild rye) once formed the base of our historical grasslands, imported pasture grasses such as smooth brome, orchard grass, and quack grass have elbowed them out to dominate the landscapes of the field today.

These wildflowers and grasses of the field quickly cover the ground in the first years following disturbance, protecting it from the sun's heat, drying winds, soil erosion, and nutrient loss. Together, these plants provide pollen, nectar, foliage, seeds, and cover that invite insects and small mammals to the area. This creates the basis of a more complex food web. In time, woody plants move in.

The first woody plants to grow in the field are often shrubs and small trees. Of these first responders, none work harder than the native shrubs gray dogwood and staghorn sumac. Berry-eating birds have spread gray dogwood and staghorn sumac to every corner of the Golden Horseshoe, where they sucker through the ground to form large thickets.

Wild crabapple in flower on a woodland edge near Waterdown.

Other small trees of the field include a range of colourful native fruit trees such as American plum, Canada plum, wild crabapple, and pin cherry. When I began my tree study, it took me a few years to spot these small trees as they are easily overlooked when not in flower.

Apples and pears are also common in the fields of the Golden Horseshoe. They have their origins in the

American plum in flower at the Mississaugas of the New Credit Pow Wow Grounds. **(inset)** American plums on a roadside near Cayuga.

Old World but have been grown here for more than two hundred years. They persist in abandoned orchards and are spread by feeding mammals, including humans. The late Ed Voss, author of *Michigan Flora*, wrote: "Human beings discarding cores are doubtless a major agent of dispersal."

And then there are the hawthorns. These scrappy little trees of thickets, hedgerows, and open woodlands are notorious for hybridizing, making identification of individual species difficult. Hawthorns are not only our most diverse native trees — about twenty-five different species are found in the Golden Horseshoe alone — they also take the prize for our most prickly native trees, as they are armed with numerous sharp thorns. Some of the more common species in the Golden Horseshoe include downy, dotted, and cockspur hawthorn.

Together, the shrubs and small trees of the field create dense thickets that provide feeding areas, hiding places, and travel corridors for a variety of wildlife, including birds, rabbits, snakes, foxes, and coyotes — as well as shelter for boys escaping barking dogs.

The largest trees that colonize field habitats are called pioneer trees because they are the first to arrive on the scene of open and disturbed habitats. Pioneer trees are fast growers and prolific seed producers. Some of the most common native pioneer trees in the Golden Horseshoe include trembling aspen, largetooth aspen, red ash, white elm, bur oak, black walnut, white pine, and red cedar. Pioneer trees create vertical diversity, attracting more climbers, leaf-eaters, perchers, and pollinators.

Black walnut and red cedar at Short Hills Provincial Park, near St. Catharines.

Together, the shrubs and trees of the field create young, messy-looking forests. Ecologists call them early successional forests.

How an early successional forest develops depends upon the quality of the surrounding habitat. An isolated, urban brownfield is more likely to attract weedy city trees like Manitoba maple, tree-of-heaven, Siberian elm, white mulberry, and buckthorn. A back-forty field surrounded by meadows,

White pine, hawthorns, teasel, tall goldenrod, and New England aster grow in a field in Mississauga.

hedgerows, and remnant woodlands will often attract native pioneer trees.

With time, the pioneer trees shade out the light-hungry grasses, wildflowers, shrubs, and small trees of the field, and their accumulated leaf fall builds soils that prepare the ground for longer-lived forest trees such as sugar maple, beech, hemlock, red oak, and white pine, as well as shrubs, sedges, ferns, and wildflowers that are tolerant of shaded forest environments. This entire process from field to young forest takes several decades depending upon the growing conditions and the amount of seed migration (by wind and wildlife) from the surrounding landscape.

I still love wandering through fields like I did when I was a kid. The sun, the wind, the open skies — there is a lightness, a freedom, in the field, and I feel drawn to its youthful spirit: the kinetic energy, the innocence and beauty, the awkward grace, the stabs at structure and search for form. They're places where I can recapture the feeling of skipping to school along those muddy trails on Sewell Drive. But today I also look to the field for insight on how to add more nature and restore ecosystem function in our urban and suburban lives.

Professor Doug Tallamy, in his book *Bringing Nature Home*, writes,

> We can no longer safely relegate nature to our parks and preserves, assured that it will be there for us when we need it. We can no longer replace the native vegetation in our neighbourhoods with foreign plants and remain confident that our native species will

> survive somewhere else. We can no longer rely on local natural areas to supply food and shelter to the birds, mammals, reptiles, and amphibians of North America.

So much of our tablelands have been converted to agriculture, asphalt, and concrete that we now have to plant our gardens with native species to restore ecosystem function in our cities and towns. Tallamy says there are three tasks we should be concentrating on to achieve that goal:

- reducing the size of our lawns and creating more native plant gardens;
- transitioning our existing plantings to natives when ornamentals die; and
- creating corridors connecting natural areas in our built landscapes.

These are all tasks perfectly suited to the trees, shrubs, perennials, and grasses of the field, as the sunny growing conditions of the field and forest edges match the sunny growing conditions found in our cities and towns. Therefore, the plants of the field can be introduced into our cities wherever there's a glut of mowed grass — which is to say everywhere from backyards and boulevards to schoolyards, parkland, and corporate parks.

Red and white ashes, buckthorn, and gray dogwood in the Berry Tract, Royal Botanical Gardens, Hamilton.

In my garden and naturalization projects, I use dozens of native wildflowers of the field, such as black-eyed Susan, butterfly milkweed, wild bergamot, sweet ox-eye, Joe-pye weed, smooth beardtongue, blue vervain, dense blazing-star, New England aster, and Virginia mountain mint.

For grassy garden textures, instead of planting commonly used exotics like miscanthus and pennisetum, I'll plant native prairie grasses such as Indian grass, little bluestem, and prairie dropseed. Instead of tired garden shrubs like lilac, forsythia, and rugosa roses that our native insects can't recognize or use, I'll plant field natives like nannyberry, American plum, and Carolina rose, which feed those insects. Instead of blue spruce and Austrian pine, I'll plant red cedar and white pine. Instead of Norway maple, horse-chestnut, and little-leaf linden, I'll plant fast-growing trees with high wildlife value, which include bur oak, black cherry, and trembling aspen.

In sprawling corporate parks, naturalized spaces can be used by employees as lunchtime retreats from the stresses of office life. In parks and boulevards, these spaces can reduce maintenance costs for municipalities. On school grounds, they can be teaching tools for students. And in between the forest islands in our rural lands, we can harness the power of the trees of the field to buffer forests and beef up habitat connections.

I've packed my small lot in downtown Hamilton with as many native trees, shrubs, wildflowers, and grasses of the field as possible, and I'm still finding

A corporate naturalization project in Sheridan Business Park, Mississauga.

ways to squeeze in more. Sitting in the garden with a cold beer and watching the bees, birds, and butterflies go about their business is endlessly entertaining. I love how I can stick my face close to these feeding insects and they just continue to buzz from flower to flower and feed — it's that same feeling I had as a kid observing the insects in the fields around Forest Hill.

By inviting the plants of the field into our cities and towns, we can combat habitat loss, create feeding areas for birds, bees, and butterflies, and bring back a little adventure for kids of all ages.

5

In the Forest

Back when I played in the McCraney Creek woods, I couldn't tell the difference between an ash, hickory, or oak, or between evergreens like white pine and hemlock. I knew the maple leaf because of our flag, and remember a few lessons on trees in elementary school that involved preserving a leaf between sheets of waxed paper with a clothes iron. Not enough for anything to sink in, for me to start thinking of trees as living, breathing things. If anything, for my friends and me, trees were things, to be used and abused.

While building our forts, we'd cut down dozens of young trees for lumber and knock nails into live trees. We'd pick up pieces of deadwood and swing them like bats against tree trunks in each other's direction — the tip of the deadwood breaking off to become a flying projectile. We could get off two or three wooden bullets before searching the ground for a new bat.

We'd hang trees, too. Hanging a tree involves climbing a sturdy sapling, grabbing it near the top with both hands and parachuting down to the ground, the tree bending in an arc under the stress. We probably hurt a lot of trees this way, but figured the trees were like us: flexible, agile, and resilient to bumps, bends, and bruises.

Things changed after I went to Sault College and began putting names to trees. As my friendship with trees grew, I became eager to learn more about them. I scoured any books on the trees of eastern North America I could find. I attended conferences, talks, and courses on the ecology and conservation of southern Ontario. I studied topographic maps of the Golden Horseshoe, seeking out forests off the beaten path that I could cut my growing botanical teeth on. In time, I started to inquire about the history of the land. I wondered about the pre-settlement past when the Golden Horseshoe was home to some of the richest temperate forests on the planet. How big did the trees get? How old did the trees become? How have the forests changed since then? Often this questioning devolved into fantasy. I even began to dream about it.

For years I had a recurring dream about walking through a village surrounded by gigantic trees. Some of the trunks were more than six feet wide and rose 150 feet into a mass of heavy, twisted limbs. Their size gave the impression of being out West, that they were Douglas firs or western red cedars. But these trees were familiar. I knew I was in southern Ontario. I knew the trees were maple, oak, and pine.

I still daydream about the primeval forests of the Golden Horseshoe, projecting the past onto the present. Sometimes I imagine the old woods while sitting in my reading chair at home — giant fluted trunks planted in my living room floor. I look at the original trees remaining in our streets and try to imagine hundreds more in a jumble of huge columns. While driving on the highway I study the rise and fall of the land between the creeks, and in my mind I pull back the asphalt, concrete, brick, and steel and try to picture how it must have looked before Cabot, Cartier, and Champlain began their voyages across the Atlantic.

Picturing the pre-settlement forests of the Golden Horseshoe is an exercise for the imagination. It requires cobbling together what little was recorded, and seeking out the pieces of magic that survive on the land today. For me, it's a way of getting a handle on the arboreal potential of my home, a way of connecting to the past in order to help shape our future forests.

EVIDENCE

Photography arrived too late to capture the old woods of the Golden Horseshoe. Paintings and sketches are the only visuals we have from that time.

Many of the earliest works are of Niagara Falls. Kriegoff's (1858) and Davies's (1766) interpretations are my favourites, reminding us that forest used to envelope Niagara Falls, not the cheap amusements that do today. Elizabeth Hale's watercolour *York* (1804) shows an early Front Street in Toronto (and the original beach line before the harbour was filled in) with nothing to the north but billowing clouds of deciduous trees pierced by the pointed spires of white pine. Sir Frederick Verner's painting *The Mill* depicts the woods along the lower Sixteen Mile Creek in Old Oakville in 1856. William Blair Bruce's *Chedoke Ravine* (1880) shows the rocky woods of Chedoke Creek in Hamilton long before it was buried and the 403 built over it.

The Mill, by Sir Frederick Verner, depicts the old woods along the lower Sixteen Mile Creek in Oakville in 1856.

I think the most captivating images of the old woods of the Golden Horseshoe were by Elizabeth Simcoe, wife of the Lieutenant Governor of Upper Canada, John Graves Simcoe, created during their time here in the 1790s. Her paintings of Toronto's Castle Frank nuzzled into the thick woods of the Don Valley are otherworldly compared to the stream of traffic that flows there today. And her watercolour *Burlington Bay* depicts the woods on the lake plain in Stoney Creek on June 10, 1796 — no houses, condo towers, office buildings, or industrial development, just a bunch of squiggly brush strokes depicting the forest canopy between the Escarpment and the lakeshore.

Elizabeth Simcoe's watercolour *Burlington Bay*, painted on June 10, 1796, from atop the Niagara Escarpment near present-day Stoney Creek. In the distance, you can see the escarpment ridge near the present-day neighbourhood of Tyandaga in Burlington (the same ridge is visible in the photo on page 69).

More insight into the size and extent of the old woods can be found by reading the descriptions of early explorers, tourists, and pioneers.

Jesuit priest Pierre Charlevoix, travelling by canoe along the north shore of Lake Erie in May 1721, wrote: "Wherever I went ashore I was quite enchanted by the beauty and variety of a landscape which was terminated by the noblest forests in the whole world."

Robert Gourlay, in his *Statistical Account of Upper Canada*, wrote: "In 1784, the whole country was one continued forest. Some plains on the borders of Lake Erie, at the head of Lake Ontario, and in a few other places, were thinly wooded: but, in general, the land in its natural state was heavily loaded with trees."

And in her travel memoir *Winter Studies and Summer Rambles in Canada*, Anna Brownell Jameson gushes about the primeval forest at the Head of the Lake during her horse-drawn carriage ride from Hamilton to Woodstock in 1837:

> No one who has a single atom of imagination can travel through these forest roads of Canada without being strongly impressed and excited. The seemingly interminable line of trees before you, the boundless wilderness around; the mysterious depths amid the multitudinous foliage, where foot of man hath never penetrated — and which partial gleams of the noontide sun, now seen, now lost, lit up with a changeful, magical beauty — the wondrous splendour and novelty of the flowers — the silence, unbroken but by the low cry of a bird, or hum of insect, or the splash and croak of some huge bull-frog — the solitude in which we proceeded mile after mile, no human being, no human dwelling within sight.... Their effect on myself I can hardly describe in words.

Even more interesting are the few descriptions of the size of individual trees in the old woods.

In 1827, early Wellington County settler John Galt recounted felling a sugar maple at Guelph with a girth of six metres, the tree falling "with a crash of accumulated thunder...." The Beverly Oak, a white oak that once stood near Cambridge, was described by Samuel Strickland in his 1853 memoir as 3.4 metres in diameter and 21 metres up to the first branch. The only reason it was kept standing was because the landowner didn't have a crosscut saw long enough to take it down.

White pines were the tallest trees in the old woods and were prized by the shipbuilders of the British Royal Navy. North of Toronto, Whitchurch-Stouffville was an active logging area in the late 1800s that was known for its pines a metre-and-a-half in diameter and forty metres tall. Samuel Thompson, an early settler on the Simcoe lowlands southwest of Barrie, described seeing "solitary pine nearly five feet thick and somewhere about a hundred and seventy feet in height." According to Hazel C. Mathews in *Oakville and the Sixteen*, another pioneer account described a white pine in the Port Credit area as follows:

(right) Soaring white pines in an old-growth forest remnant on the south shore of Cootes Paradise in Hamilton.

> Wonderful Tree — In Toronto Township near the Centre Road [Hurontario Street] there is a pine tree of immense size — perhaps the largest in this quarter of the county. About a yard from the ground it is by actual measurement twenty and one half feet in circumference and it appears to be little less for sixty of seventy feet up. Its height, as near as can be judged, is about two hundred feet. It is called Johnnie Martin's Pine Tree because he never passed without stopping to admire it.

The most detailed accounts of the old woods of the Golden Horseshoe come from the land surveys of Jones, Wilmot, Burwell, Chewett, Iredell, Stegman, and other Crown surveyors in the late 1700s and early 1800s. For each lot and concession, they recorded notes on soil fertility, physical features, and the major tree species found. Below is a list of some present-day landmarks and the trees that dominated those areas as recorded by Crown surveyors more than two hundred years ago:

- Square One, Mississauga: maple, beech, hemlock
- Mississauga City Centre: maple, oak, beech
- Canada's Wonderland, Vaughan: maple, elm, basswood

- Darlington Nuclear Generating Station, Bowmanville: maple, beech, pine, hemlock
- Toronto Financial District: pine plains
- Pearson Airport, Mississauga: maple, beech, hickory, basswood
- Mohawk Racetrack, Milton: very large pine
- Downtown Guelph: maple, beech, elm, basswood
- Ivor Wynne Stadium, Hamilton: large pine, oak, hickory
- Hamilton Airport: beech, maple, chestnut
- Brock's Monument, Niagara-on-the-Lake: oak, hickory plains

It's incredible to think that open grassy forests once occupied the Toronto Financial District, that pillars of maple, beech, and hemlock towered over the food court at Square One, and giant white pines once crowded the land where the Ticats play today.

The early artworks, the writings of the first settlers, and the descriptions of Crown surveyors are all a great help for imagining the pre-settlement forests of the Golden Horseshoe. They also remind us of how much we have lost, and how much we have altered the land over the last couple of centuries.

Today, the forests of the Golden Horseshoe are a patchwork of small, scattered back-forty woods in rural areas and isolated urban parks surrounded by suburban, retail, and industrial development. Our largest forests put up a fight by their difficult terrain: the complex topographies of the Dundas Valley, Short Hills, and Oak Ridges Moraine, the rocky woods of the Niagara Escarpment, and the ribbons of green along our creek valleys.

In pre-settlement times, about 80 percent of the Golden Horseshoe was forested, the remainder being wetlands, savannahs, and prairies. Today, our forest cover hovers around 15 percent. The glaring exception to this is the 30 percent forest cover found at Six Nations and the Mississaugas of the New Credit south of Brantford, a block of land that provides such a contrast to the surrounding landscape that it's visible from space.

Besides the loss of big trees, the composition of our remaining forests has changed over the last two centuries. Sure, most of the major components are still there — the beech, sugar maple, red oak, white oak, shagbark hickory, white pine, and others — but much has been lost along the way.

Early Crown surveyors listed white elm and basswood as common companions of beech and sugar maple in the old woods. Today, basswood is at best a secondary species, and large trees are few and far between. And since the arrival of Dutch elm disease, forest-grown, canopy-height white elms have gone the way of the dodo; white elm is now a minor tree of fields and swamps.

Our native chestnut was also a prominent tree in the old woods of the Golden Horseshoe, where it grew with oak, hickory, and pine. Two hundred years ago, large stands of chestnut were found on the sands of Oakville, Burlington, Ancaster, Dundas, Glen Morris, Paris, Dunnville, Delhi, Fonthill, and Niagara Falls. Back then, "chestnuting" was a popular pastime as the nuts were sweet and nutritious, and early settlers would collect them by the bushel each autumn — a winter survival tip they learned from the First Nations. When Asian chestnut blight arrived in the 1920s, millions of chestnut trees were wiped off the landscape. Today, only a few hundred trees remain in the Golden Horseshoe, most still suffering the effects of the blight.

In recent years, we've been losing more of our forest trees to imported pests and disease: the beech to bark disease, the butternut to canker, and the white ash to emerald ash borer. The jury is still out on whether other pests and diseases will harm more forest trees in the Golden Horseshoe. Hemlock woolly adelgid, a destructive

A large open-grown black oak at Paradise Grove, Niagara-on-the-Lake.

non-native insect that has been decimating hemlock populations in the northeastern United States, has recently been found in Etobicoke and the Niagara Gorge, and there are fears that oak diseases (oak wilt and sudden oak death) will spread throughout the oak forests of the eastern United States, including southern Ontario.

Today's small forest islands are not only vulnerable to pest and disease infestation, but also to colonization by invasive plant species. Exotic plant species like garlic mustard and dog-strangling vine can be found in the ground layer of almost every remnant forest in the Golden Horseshoe. In the shrub layer, European buckthorn and weedy honeysuckles elbow out the chokecherries, serviceberries, dogwoods, witch-hazels, and viburnums. In the canopy, Norway maple is often seen competing with our native sugar maple for light and nutrients, especially in urban forests where their seeds blow through streets, float into catch basins, and twirl into ravines. I've been in some forests in Toronto that

(left) Old trees aren't always large trees. A stunted white oak grows on the edge of a slough at Grassie in Niagara Region. Its age? Two hundred and ninety-five years.
(right) Beyond the stunted white cedars of the Niagara Escarpment, the next oldest trees in the Golden Horseshoe would be black gums found in the slough forests of Niagara Region. Arborist Nate Torenvliet stands beside the 580-year-old black gum near Fort Erie that he aged with an increment borer.

have complete non-native floral suites: Norway maple/Siberian elm canopies, tatarian honeysuckle shrub layers, and garlic mustard/dog-strangling vine ground layers.

The problem is compounded by the high traffic in our remaining urban forests as weed seed is tracked in on city truck tires, bicycles, ATVs, shoe soles, and dogs. All the while, surplus deer and wild turkey populations busily over-graze the remaining native ground flora. Sometimes I can't help but think the preponderance of the native poison ivy vine in our disturbed woodlands could be viewed as a "Piss Off!" from the land.

To add insult to injury, we are still losing forests.

According to the Carolinian Canada Coalition, even after all the increased awareness around habitat conservation in recent decades, natural cover in the Golden Horseshoe continued to drop between 2000 and 2010. And hardwood harvests continue with regularity in many private forests across the Golden Horseshoe. When trees reach a harvestable age, say eighty to one hundred and twenty-five years, they are quickly plucked and dispatched to the sawmill for quick profit. Remember, these are trees that can live three hundred, four hundred, even five hundred years. To chop down every hundred-year-old tree is like sending high-school grads to the guillotine.

Our forests have many challenges, but they don't discourage me from getting out and exploring. If

(top) Staring up into the canopy of an old-growth forest remnant, Ancaster, Ontario.
(bottom) Long, limbless boles of old-growth hemlock, sugar maple, and red oak at Homer Watson Park in Kitchener.

anything, it just makes me want to try harder to seek out our remaining older and high-quality forests in order to piece together a picture of our arboreal past.

Most days I don't see anything to add to that picture. But the more you look, the more you see — an ancient ravine slope, a hectare or two hemmed in by complex topography, a forgotten corner, a few old souls standing stalwart among the youth.

After twenty-five years of forest study, forest dreaming, and forest imagining, I still feel that I have a poor understanding of the old woods of the Golden Horseshoe. Too little was recorded; too little has been left. There are so many plants and animals that, because of habitat destruction, no longer occur in the Golden Horseshoe: plants such as white milkweed, twisted sedge, fairy wand, the downy gentian, Bowman's root, and rose-pink; the southern cloudywing, tawny crescent, and karner blue butterflies; and bird species such as the piping plover, king rail, and loggerhead shrike.

All of these species supported a network of other species. So, we can't just count the loss of individual species. We must also account for the lost interactions, connections, nuances, and magic with other species. For the sum is greater than the individual parts.

There's no doubt that the network of life and all the possible biological interactions between species in the great old woods of the Golden Horseshoe was astoundingly rich. This natural richness filled the forests of the past and was very familiar to the First Nations of the Golden Horseshoe. Being dazzled by the diversity of their surroundings was part of their everyday experience and it shaped their beliefs and ceremony. This forest magic — that woodsy calm — was something we were all meant to experience and be inspired by.

Today, half of the remaining 1,300 or so native plants of the Golden Horseshoe are rare, with dozens on the brink of extirpation. We can't afford to lose any more plants, any more magic. Now more than ever we must save every connection. We must find a new balance, a new arboreal potential for the forests of the Golden Horseshoe.

Forest researchers talk about the 30 percent factor: to maintain healthy watersheds for wildlife, including humans, we need to retain a minimum of 30 percent forest cover. So, our path in the Golden Horseshoe is clear: we must double our forest cover.

Fortunately, our native trees are ready to help. We need to harness the healing power of the trees of the

(left) Tuliptrees in the Niagara Glen Nature Reserve, an old-growth forest in the Niagara Gorge.
(right) Three-hundred-year-old beech trees at Jackson-Gunn Old Growth Forest, Norfolk County.

field to build new forests. We need to plant the trembling aspen, red cedar, gray dogwood, hawthorns, pin cherries, and plums to prepare the ground for the red oak, white oak, shagbark hickory, white pine, hemlock, sugar maple, beech, and tuliptree.

As I wrote at the end of chapter 3, we all need to become modern Johnny Appleseeds, planting acorns and hickory nuts in backyards, school grounds, parks, roadsides, turnpikes, and any other marginal lands to create groves of productive native trees to support local biodiversity. Urban forests like the McCraney Creek woods can be improved by controlling invasive species, beefing up the forest edges through volunteer plantings, and planting more native forest trees in the neighbourhoods around it.

There is much creative energy already working toward these goals: community groups that host volunteer plantings and garbage cleanups, rural landowners planting marginal lands through government incentive programs, and progressive municipalities working to restore degraded ravines by removing invasive species and planting native trees. But to double our forest cover, these efforts need to be extended throughout every neighbourhood in the Golden Horseshoe. It's a lot of work, but the rewards will be great.

We'll never truly know what the old woods of the Golden Horseshoe were like. But through these efforts there can come a day when our descendants can imagine the old woods with greater clarity. They'll be able to walk out their front doors to boulevards filled with our native forest trees, neighbourhoods with healthy urban forests, and a web of green that stretches across the entire Golden Horseshoe.

6

On the Water

I grew up Roman Catholic — baptized, confirmed, Catholic school, the works. I never enjoyed going to church, especially those Easter masses that, by the third hour, hurt my legs with the incessant standing, sitting, and kneeling. As a ten-year-old, when asked by my teacher if I wanted to be an altar boy, I answered with a decisive, "No, thank you."

About the only things I didn't mind about growing up as a churchgoer were the monthly Masses in high school (they gave me a break from class); my grade eleven world religion class, which gave me at least a partial view of spirituality outside of Catholicism; and reciting my bedtime prayers, which I had turned into a game, saying them as quickly as I could like one of those fast talkers on TV listing the side effects of some medication: *I lay my body down to sleep, I pray to God my soul to keep, and if I die before I wake, I pray to God my soul to take. God bless Patrick, Deirdre, Mommy, and Daddy, all my relations and friends and you I promise to pray for*. I can still rhyme it off with emotionless efficiency to this day.

During my preteens, my mom used to send my brother and me to Sunday Mass at St. Mike's, the church beside our elementary school. Sometimes we'd fool our friend Lee into coming along with us. "Come on, it'll be fun," my brother would say. "It's only an hour and then we can go play," I would echo. After fooling him a couple times, Lee quickly realized that Mass *wasn't* going to be fun and that that hour would be the longest of his life; he never came to Mass with us again.

Soon my brother started skipping out.

Oh, he'd walk out the front door of our house and feign like he was going. Sometimes he'd even get as far as the church doors to pick up a program. But once he had that golden ticket in his hands, he'd head over to a friend's house, leaving me to sit in the pew by myself.

This went on for several months, me going to Mass, my brother skipping out. Soon I began crafting ways of shortening the painful hour. I started to walk in late and sit at the back. I'd leave before closing prayers, tonguing the host like a toad and hopping out the side exit. Finally, I started to skip out entirely and wait the hour out along the banks of McCraney Creek.

Sitting beside the creek and staring into its shallow flow was a much more calming and divine experience than anything I felt in church. Plus, it was the outdoors. It was tangible. It was something I could believe in. Outside was where all the things Father Mihm talked about in mass: life, beauty, spirit.

Eventually, my brother and I told my mom that we didn't want to go to church anymore, and thankfully, she didn't press us.

Life was changing fast by the time I hit my teens. I started high school, my parents had separated, and my mom, brother, sister, and I moved out of our house on Forest Hill into a townhouse around the corner on Eton Place on the edge of the Morrison Creek valley. It was hard leaving my childhood home. We had lived there for eight years. But at least the arguments stopped and, most importantly, at least we stayed on the hill.

By grade ten, I went from staying in Friday nights to watch *The A-Team* to standing in front of the liquor store at Oakville Place with half a dozen friends until one of us worked up the nerve to approach an adult we thought might be "cool." Our booty secured — a five-dollar six-pack of Old Milwaukee each — we'd head across the fields of Oakville Town Hall to a spot on the Morrison Creek we called "The Bridge."

The Bridge is where Morrison Creek meets the base of Trafalgar Road hill, just steps away from where the ancient trail once ran. It's a concrete platform that the Morrison flows under before it enters the Morrison Wedgewood Diversion Channel and is funnelled west toward the Sixteen. We named it that because, well, it's a bridge, but also because of "The Crunge" — the Led Zeppelin song that has Plant pleading in the outro, "Has anybody seen the bridge?!"

As you might have guessed, we weren't in with the popular crowd in high school. We were never invited to their parties and only rarely did we attend the school dances. About the only parties we did go to were the outdoor ones — the bush parties. The popular bush party spot was on a precipice on the east side of the Sixteen Mile Creek just north of Upper Middle Road, where, by midnight, there'd be a hundred high school kids drinking beer and smoking joints around a raging bonfire.

But most Friday and Saturday nights during our teens you could find our gang in our own little world partying down at The Bridge, even on the coldest winter nights.

We thought we were really clever all cozied up behind the Cop Shop less than a hundred metres away, but that didn't stop an officer from strolling down the valley a couple of times to confiscate our beers and give us all "fifty-threes" (fifty-three-dollar fines) for underage drinking.

Summertime at The Bridge was the best, when the evening air was warm and we could don T-shirts and shorts and sit on the edge of the concrete lip of The Bridge, sipping our beers without getting cold bums. One magical summer evening we witnessed the mass flight of cicadas from the trees in the Morrison Creek valley. It was a beautiful sight: the hot orange of the late sinking sun, the sky filled with the buzzing of thousands of peanut-sized insects, and us hosers dancing among them hooting and hollering, beers in hand.

The Bridge was also the place where we experimented with altered states beyond the beer. It was the first

(right) The Oakville portion of the 1877 Halton County map. "Trafalgar," at the top right, is the present-day Uptown Core at Trafalgar Road and Dundas Street. The arrows show where springs (SPRING or SP) are located on the map. Freshwater springs were common along every creek and river in the Golden Horseshoe in pre-settlement times.

TRAFALGAR
MUNN'S COR
GREAT WESTERN RY
STATION
OAKVILLE
ONTARIO

place we smoked hash, dropped acid, and tried magic mushrooms. Say what you will, but in the absence of a rite of passage for boys growing up in the Golden Horseshoe, we created our own. I know my confirmation was supposed to symbolize some kind of rite of passage, but for me the experience fell flat. It was something I was told by adults: choose a name, put on a tie and jacket, and walk down the church aisle to pick up a piece of paper.

Our rite of passage at The Bridge was exactly that — it was *ours*. It was, I believe, like we were instinctively scrambling toward the desire shared by many human cultures the world over: to look to nature as a guide for personal growth. Our misguided rite of passage at The Bridge wasn't something each of us did solo, and I can't say we saw some special sign from the land or experienced something beyond ourselves, other than that magical evening when we witnessed the Dance of the Cicadas. But it was a place where we tested the waters on our own terms. It wasn't about the beer and the drugs. It was about being outside, away from the scrutiny of adults, about doing our own thing, about navigating the spiritual bridge between adolescence and adulthood, the trickle of the Morrison a constant note beneath our feet.

The Bridge today. Our graffiti has been long painted over by its new youth stewards.

A cottonwood flowers in early spring along the Grindstone Creek in Burlington.

Standing at The Bridge today, Morrison Creek may not look like much. It flows year-round, but mostly it's just a dribble. The only time it courses with any power is during the spring runoff, when you might get your knees wet. But, just as we must look at the trees in our remnant forests today and double and triple their height and girth to imagine the grandeur of our original forests, we must imbue our creeks and rivers with much greater power and spirit to imagine them when they ran wild and free and true only a few generations ago. As E.C. Guillet wrote in *Pioneer Travel in Upper Canada* (1933),

> It must be remembered … that the streams of today have much less water than they had in the days of the fur trade and early settlement. The clearing of the forests from the face of the land has led to the quick evaporation or drainage of the surface water, and many a noble river has shrunk to a mere creek …

And before the St. Lawrence Seaway regulated lake levels, Lake Ontario heaved with the ferocity of a sea. According to an 1820 government report cited in *Burlington Bay, Beach and Heights, in History*, by Mary Rose Holden, in 1898,

> during the Spring and Fall seasons, "Ocean Winds," as they were called by old mariners, rose, causing the waters of the Lake to rise and fall in intensity and velocity with that of the Atlantic, rushing through the cut [the Desjardin Canal in Hamilton Harbour] at a velocity of between six and seven miles an hour, forming a tide in the Bay, raising the waters round the shores, flooding Coot's Paradise, above, almost to the town of Dundas, so that when the storm abated the pent up waters returned to the Lake with a similar velocity.

The First Nations of the Golden Horseshoe knew well the power of the water. They chose their river fords with care and only crossed when it was safe to do so. Their forest pathways skirted around swamps, since swamps were not only difficult places to walk through, but also easy places to get lost in. Some early European settlers didn't take as much heed of the power of the water and there are many stories in county histories of colonists getting lost in wetland habitats.

One of the most memorable of these stories for me concerns an early settler who got lost in the winter woods on a walk from Bowmanville to Emily

Township, west of Peterborough. He decided to take a shortcut home through a cedar swamp instead of taking the longer, tried and true route by road. He made good progress for the first half of his journey while following a sleigh track, but then a snowstorm blew in and obscured his path. Having gotten turned around, he had to bed down for the night in the swamp.

He found a dry spot, built a temporary shelter with some hemlock brush, collected some firewood and built a small fire with the "punk" (punky wood that every backwoodsman would carry around back then to use as a fire-starter) he carried, and ate the small rations he had brought. The next morning was clear and he started out once more. But the snow soon returned. By late afternoon, his spirits began to rise as he found the fresh tracks of a man he assumed was probably out hunting for deer. He followed the tracks for some time until, an hour before dark, he came upon a smouldering fire. To his dismay, he discovered that they were his own tracks that he had been following and that the fire was his own from the previous night. He had turned in a complete circle. He had to bed down in the woods again, this time without a fire because his punk had gotten wet from the snow.

The next morning, with his remaining energies, he walked on and after some time heard a cock crowing in

Black willows on the Twenty Mile Creek in Hamilton Region.

the distance. He yelled out. Some neighbours heard his calls and later found his nearly lifeless body and took him home. Unfortunately, they made the mistake of putting his frostbitten form in front of the fire (instead of thawing him out more slowly) and he died the next week.

First Nations travellers also knew to hug the shoreline rather than to strike out across the open water when paddling their elm bark canoes on Lake Ontario. Early settlers followed the lead of Indigenous Peoples and named many of our creeks from this travel practice — the Two, Four, Eight, Twelve, Fifteen, Sixteen, Thirty, and Forty Mile Creeks in Niagara Region are named for their distance from the Niagara River; the Twelve (Bronte), Fourteen, and Sixteen Mile Creeks in Oakville are named for their distance from the Head of the Lake.

For Indigenous Peoples, reverence and respect for water was a profound component of their faith. Both the Haudenosaunee and Anishinaabeg of the Golden Horseshoe believed — and in some cases still believe — in the animistic view that water was more akin to a "Being" than the Eurocentric view that classifies it as a mere "thing."

The dozens of waterfalls that spill over the Escarpment were met with reverence and offerings of tobacco, especially at Niagara, where the master of all the waterfalls was said to reside. The density of archaeological sites in the region suggests that the area was special.

For the Anishinaabeg, the Toronto Islands were known as Menecing, a place of healing where the sick would go to rest on its beaches and sheltered lagoons.

The spring that flows from the bank of the Grand River at Homer Watson Park in south Kitchener tells the legend of Oromocto Spring. It's a love story between

Oromocto, a Petun warrior, and Nashwaaksis, a woman from the Neutral Confederacy. Oromocto was killed by an Iroquois hunting party and Nashwaaksis, unable to contain her grief, fell dead upon him. A Neutral search party found the pair two days later, and when they lifted them up, a spring of water gushed out of the ground as testament to their love.

Lake Medad in Waterdown was a gathering area for the Mississauga, and before them, a village site for the Neutrals for many years. There are old stories about the lake being bottomless or connected to Lake Ontario, and that the lake sometimes gave off booming or explosion-like sounds.

The Mississauga told tales of serpents that lived in Lake Ontario, and a Mississauga Chief on a white horse that haunted the lower Bronte Creek. And there were friendly, mischievous fairies or elves — or Mamagwasewug — that lived among them along riverbanks and in wetlands. In *Sacred Feathers* (1987), Professor Donald B. Smith writes:

> The Mamagwasewug or elves were small friendly beings who might play tricks on humans but never harmed them. Although invisible, the little creatures could show themselves. Many elders had

> talked to these strange beings, who stood about a metre high. Walking erect, they had a human form but their faces were covered with short hair. The elves loved shooting off guns they had stolen from the Indians or taken from graves. Often the Indians heard them in a large pond near Burlington Bay. Here some elders had once seen them paddling a stone canoe, but when they gave chase they quickly crossed over to a high bank and disappeared. After they vanished nothing could be heard but a distant rumbling. Another tribe of Mamagwasewug lived, the old people said, on the east bank of the Credit River, nearly two kilometres from the lake.

And then there is the Anishinaabeg story of the Munedoo, retold by Peter Jones (Sacred Feathers) in his 1861 book *History of the Ojebway Indians*:

> Near the Credit Village, at the foot of a pointed hill, is a deep hole in the water, which is said to be the abode of one of the water-gods, where he was frequently heard to sing and beat his drum. When the white

> people began to frequent this place for the purpose of taking salmon, this Munedoo took his departure during a tremendous flood caused by his power, and went down the river into Lake Ontario.

Elves paddling stone canoes, serpents in Lake Ontario, a water-god that lived in the Credit River … to modern ears these stories sound fantastical, but again, they were born at a time when Lake Ontario and our rivers were more powerful, more magical, and the human connection to the water was stronger and more visceral.

Sacred Feathers described the stories of the elves and the Munedoo. Born in 1802, Sacred Feathers stood between two worlds: he was Peter Jones, the son of Welsh surveyor Augustus Jones and Tuhbenahneequay, daughter of the Mississauga chief Wahbanosay. He was brought up among First Nations people in the wilderness of Hamilton Harbour, and later attended the schools of the English along the Grand River. Sacred Feathers was bilingual and bicultural, and although he became a Methodist minister, he never forgot his Anishinaabeg roots.

(left) A trio of black walnuts in the Bronte Creek floodplain in Oakville.

As a boy in the early 1800s, Sacred Feathers rose before dawn, blackened his face with charcoal, and walked off into the forests of the Burlington Heights for his Vision Quest. The elders told him to pay attention to the land — every notable dream, event, and sound — to experience his vision. I imagine him sitting on a hill somewhere on the edge of Cootes Paradise, maybe at Sassafras Point, resting on a shag carpet of Pennsylvania sedge among scattered black oaks and looking out over the beds of wild rice that once covered the coastal marsh. He sat fasting for days. But he didn't see anything. No spirit animal. No sign from the sky. No Manitou that visited his dreams. Sacred Feathers went on many Vision Quests as a youth, but never had a vision.

Was Sacred Feathers too affected by the Methodism he was beginning to study and eventually preached in his adult years? Or did he become aware at that early age that the spirit of the land was being weakened?

Since that time, our creeks and rivers have lost much of their aquatic life. Lake Ontario has been soured with industrial chemicals, raw sewage, and invasive species, and we've lost over 80 percent of our historical wetlands — the marshes, bogs, fens, swamps, and slough forests that soak up the rain and keep our water clean.

I wonder what Sacred Feathers would think about the Golden Horseshoe today. Perhaps he'd be impressed

A large original sycamore grows in the floodplain of the Credit River at the Mississauga Golf and Country Club.

(upper left) A tamarack in fall colour at the Fletcher Creek Ecological Preserve near Morriston.
(upper right) Peachleaf willows on the Fairchild Creek in Hamilton. The perched roots show the high-water mark.
(lower left) The fall colour of a poison sumac at Ruthven Park near Cayuga.
(lower right) The leaves and stalked acorns of swamp white oak, Norfolk County.

with our industry, but also outraged by the loss of habitat. Intuitively, he'd see how spiritually impoverished the land has become, but he would also know that the spirits of the land are still there.

He'd know not to look for the Munedoo at The Pointed Hill; that he's still out there in the depths of Lake Ontario, where it's been for nearly two centuries. And as for the other spirits? The Manitous? The elves? I think he'd know that they've retreated deep into the remaining wetlands of the Golden Horseshoe, where they can live in peace and quiet, well away from our houses, high-rises, and highways, where the two-leggeds can't easily go, where the trees walk on the water.

These are places where the silver maple, black willow, peach-leaf willow, white elm, and black ash stand in the deciduous swamps, and where the black spruce, balsam fir, and tamarack huddle in the conifer swamps. Where the buttonbush, poison sumac, speckled alder, and shrub willows float in thicket swamps, and the black maple, black walnut, red elm, and sycamore gather in floodplains. Where the tall cottonwoods and balsam poplar sway on beaches, and the red ash, swamp white oak, and black gum brood in slough forests: In Cootes Paradise, Luther Marsh, and Wainfleet Bog. In Beverly Swamp, Belfountain, and the Blue Springs. In the kettle lakes of the Oak Ridges Moraine, the

A silver maple swamp in spring, Guelph Junction Woods, Halton Region.

sloughs of Caistor-Canborough, and the un-dredged coastal marshes of Durham. At Point Abino, Guelph Junction Woods, and on the Boston and McKenzie through New Credit and Six Nations. In Humberstone Marsh and Hockley Valley, Navy Island and the Nonquon. In the Niagara Gorge, the floodplains of the Grand River and, also, in the depths of Lake Ontario.

I try to be aware of the water when travelling through the Golden Horseshoe. In the mass of asphalt, metal, and concrete, I want to know where the water flows, even the smallest of brooks. It's a way of acknowledging, of honouring the spirits that live or lived there, the spirits that might one day return.

Driving on the 401 through the city of Toronto, I try to safely take in the vistas over the Etobicoke, Humber, West Don, East Don, and Rouge Rivers. Farther east, I attempt to spot the crossings of the smaller creeks through Durham Region — the Duffins, Lynde, Oshawa, Black, Harmony, Farewell, Bowmanville, and Wilmot.

On the 403 west through Aldershot, I sneak a peek down Hidden Valley, where the Grindstone flows, and then soak up the wide panorama of the wooded hills over Cootes Paradise. When I travel farther west on the 403 toward Brantford, I nod my head to the Fairchild Creek and marvel at the mighty Grand River.

On the Niagara-bound Q.E.W., I scan the deep lagoons of the Fifteen and Sixteen Mile Creeks, peer across Martindale Pond, and watch for the hop across the Chippawa Creek on the way to Fort Erie.

Travelling along the Q.E.W. east through Burlington, I keep watch for the ditches that show where the Falcon, Indian, Hager-Rambo, Roseland, Tuck, Shoreacres, Appleby, and Sheldon Creeks flow — much of their lengths now driven underground. I spy

White cedar, black spruce, tamarack, white elm, and red maple on the Zephyr Creek, Durham Region.

the chalky silhouettes of the sycamores in the Bronte valley, and the oak and pine that cling to the shale cliffs above the hog's back at the Sixteen.

At Trafalgar Road, of course, I look north to Forest Hill. The white pine spires that peek above the forest canopy east of the apartment buildings show where the site of The Bridge is, where decades ago McCraney and Morrison Creeks used to meet and The Old Trail used to run.

At the 403 split, I pass over Joshua Creek, which flows through east Oakville, then over Sheridan Creek, which feeds Rattray Marsh in Clarkson. Beyond Erin Mills Parkway, the slow descent to the Credit River begins, and at the signs for Mississauga Road, I know I'm getting close. And then I'm over the Credit and I have to make a choice of which way to look: north or south. There isn't enough time for both.

If I look south, I think about the elves that were said to live there. Sometimes I see rowers out practising on early mornings and wonder if they've ever seen them. But most times when crossing the Credit, I look north to The Pointed Hill and think about the Munedoo and wonder when, if, he will return to sing and beat his drum.

7

On the Path

I'm lucky to have been able to build a career in ecology on my own terms. It's been a tough slog, and I ain't gettin' rich, but for the most part the work is rewarding, non-stressful, and it helps to keep me balanced and close to the land. The seasonal aspect of my small business is also a big perk.

(left) The Old Indian Trail-Marker Tree, Townline Road, Thorold.

In the spring, I'm flush with energy as my work season ramps up. In late spring and summer, I'm up to cruising speed as I knock off garden and naturalization jobs and do the bulk of my habitat inventory work. In late summer and early fall, I'm still busy with botany and landscape work, but I can feel the season starting to wane. In late fall and winter, I really start to slow down. I use this time for report writing but also to daydream and follow my curiosity. Winter is also a great time for exploring the land as the subzero temperatures keep the ticks at bay. The land is quieter and more contemplative. The sightlines are longer so I can peer deeper into the structure of the woods.

One winter more than ten years ago, while following my curiosity, I discovered something that set my imagination spiralling down another path. I was scanning the Niagara Falls online digital library when I saw a photograph that has been burned into my brain to this day. It was labelled:

The Old Indian Trail-Marker Tree,
Townline Rd. (at Thorold–Stamford)

The photo (see page 162) shows a large roadside white elm on the Haldimand Clay Plain near Thorold with its side branches pulled down, the trunk and main branches drawing the shape of an *M*, the lateral branches forming the crown. It was said that Indigenous People from the area had purposefully modified the tree at one time — in the early to mid-1800s, I would guess — to point along the old Mohawk Trail, which ran along the top of the escarpment from Niagara to Hamilton. The tree was well known in the community and had been ravaged by Dutch elm disease in the early 1970s, but was saved as a snag until a windstorm in December of 1982 finally brought it down.

Wow, I thought, dumbfounded and flooded with questions. Where do I find out more about Indigenous trail marker trees? Are they really pointing along trails? Are there more photos I could find? Are there marker trees standing on the landscape of southern Ontario today? Were there trees that marked the ancient trail below Trafalgar Road hill a couple of centuries ago?

During a quick online search, I came across a couple of sites about marker trees (both from the United States) and ordered their books. The first site is run by the Mountain Stewards of the Southern Appalachians; the second is a link to the Great Lakes Trail Marker Tree Society. Both sites showed numerous photos of trail marker trees standing in the U.S. today, but most of them didn't look like the Old Indian Trail-Marker Tree in Thorold. Most were modified to point in one direction and, not surprisingly, in the United States most of them were oaks.

The books described how marker trees were thought to be formed: a sapling was bent over a metre or so above ground level and its leader was tied down with rawhide or grapevine, or secured with heavy rocks. The lateral branch pointing directly upward was retained while the rest were removed. Over time the tree settled into the bend, the rawhide was removed or withered away, and a "nose" was often left to point the way. As the tree grew, the diameter of the main trunk remained larger than the lateral branch forming the crown.

It is said that marker trees were used by First Nations as exit signs off of main trails to point to all kinds of things: villages and camps, water sources and river fords, food and medicine gathering areas, or to mark boundaries between First Nations. Apparently, trail marker trees were common in pre-settlement times, but most are now lost to habitat destruction and the practice of removing ill-formed trees from woodlots.

My quest to find marker trees in southern Ontario led me to spend a winter revisiting my old haunts in Hamilton, Halton, and Niagara Regions, but to no avail. I started researching First Nations trails and walking the area along those trails — at least, anywhere there was still some forest left — to see if I might find any marker trees. I reached out to friends and colleagues, and wrote a couple of articles about marker trees for the Field Botanists of Ontario newsletter highlighting some of my research thus far. I asked club members to please contact me if they knew of any marker trees, either historical or still standing today. I got calls and emails from tree enthusiasts from across southern Ontario and spent a few years following up on them. Some of the leads were dead ends, but some led me to the most magical trees I have ever seen.

What follows is a photo gallery of the most compelling trees I documented in and around the Greater Golden Horseshoe.

On the Berry Gathering Trail

I stumbled upon this tree along Fairchild Creek north of Hamilton. It points east along the creek toward the heart of Beverly Swamp. While fawning over this rugged old sugar maple, it triggered a remembrance of a quote I once read:

Fairchild's Creek used to be a prominent Indian trail, and the Indians used to come up north for the purpose of gathering fruit …

— Letter to J.H. Smith, president of the Wentworth Historical Society, from Oscar Main. Dated January 7, 1914, Wentworth Historical Society, Papers and Records, 1915, Volume Six.

Williams Family Marker

The Williams family contacted me about this large sugar maple on their rural property in Wellington County near Rockwood. The tree points parallel along the edge of a swampy valley with springs. The Williams showed me an active spring less than one hundred metres from the tree.

Wainfleet Marker

Mr. Jim Farr and the Wainfleet bur oak marker on his family farm in Niagara Region. Mr. Farr told me that his father showed him the tree when he was a boy in the late 1930s, and that it was already a large tree then. According to the *Chronicles of Wainfleet Township*, the tree marked a First Nations trail that ran between Dunnville and Effingham.

The Looping Tree

My friend Martha Howatt showed me this tree near Caledonia several years ago. This tree is unlike any I have ever seen before and I was beside myself with excitement when I first saw it. It's an old sugar maple that has been modified to turn in a complete loop — from grounded trunk to long span to anaconda-like body to upright trunk reaching into the shallow canopy of this disturbed woodland.

This amazing tree is along (or near) an old trail that can be seen on the *Map of the Niagara District in Upper Canada* drawn by Lieutenant W.A. Nesfield in 1815 (*Ontario History in Maps* by Gentilcore and Head). On the map, the trail is labelled "Indian Path" and crosses the Grand River south of Caledonia.

Twisted Red Oak

The Knechtel family showed me this strange, twisted red oak on their family farm near Stratford. The tree lies at the headwaters of the Grand and Thames Rivers and the ground around it is springy. According to the *History of Perth County to 1967*, this area was a hunting and gathering area for the First Nations of southern Ontario, from time immemorial to the early 1900s.

Milton White Elm Markers

This tree (top right) was a curiosity for Milton residents throughout the twentieth century. It stood on the east side of Highway 25, north of Sideroad 5. Joyce Reddoch read my first article in the Field Botanists of Ontario newsletter and shared this photograph with me in 2011. Her father, George Vincent Dunston, took this photo of her with the tree on July 25, 1957.

This bent white elm (bottom right) was photographed by the late Dr. Jaquith, probably in the 1950s. He labelled the slide "Bent Marker Tree near Milton." He and his wife, Barbara, lived near Terra Cotta and travelled widely from the 1940s to 1970s. Based on the position of the Niagara Escarpment in the background, biologist Bill McIlveen thinks the tree used to stand on Sideroad 10 west of 5th Line.

Both trees are long dead, but point along (or near) the First Nations path that ran beneath the Escarpment through Milton; the trail ran from Hamilton to Barrie.

Norfolk Beech Marker

Shirley Rothery and the unusual beech growing near her property in Norfolk County. The tree points along a tributary of the Dedrich-Young Creek where, according to Pearce's *Historical Highlights of Norfolk County*, a First Nations trail used to run.

Rice Lake Marker

This red oak in Northumberland County was shown to me by Whitney Lake and Jeff Beaver of the Alderville First Nation. That's Jeff Beaver standing beside the tree, which points north to Curtis Point on the south shore of Rice Lake.

Sixteen Mile Sugar Maples

In 1806, Crown surveyor Samuel Wilmot documented the First Nations trails that ran along the valley edges of the Sixteen Mile Creek. In 2012, I decided to retrace his steps, and found this peculiar-looking sugar maple. The tree points north along the west side of the Sixteen between Oakville and Milton.

The History of Marker Trees

There's no doubt that the marker trees shown are all really impressive trees. They are old trees with tons of character. But are they really marker trees? And, is there such a thing? Were these trees really modified by the First Nations that lived here? I always retained a tiny bit of skepticism about marker trees. That skepticism fuelled more research as I began to read county histories and the accounts of early travellers in southern Ontario, looking for any reference to marker trees. Check out these chestnuts:

> My path was a winding Indian trail where no wheel carriage had ever passed. I was obliged to jump my horse over logs, ride him through deep mud holes, and bridgeless streams, **guided sometimes by marked trees**. [September 28, 1824, near Peterborough]
>
> — *The Life and Times of the Reverend Anson Green* (1877)

> We had to go twenty miles without seeing a house and were **guided by marked trees**, there being no roads. [North shore of Lake Ontario]
>
> — *Case and His Contemporaries*, by John Carroll (1867)

> On one occasion he was **guided by marked trees**, sometimes seeing wolves cross the path before him. [Near Sherbrooke, Quebec]
>
> — *The Canadian Biographical Dictionary* (1880)

> Among the associates was Mr. John French, who in 1797 with his two elder sons, penetrated the wilderness on foot, **guided by marked trees**, for the purpose of choosing a location for settlement.
>
> — *History of the Eastern Townships, Quebec,* by C.M. Day (1869)

But a "marked tree" doesn't necessarily mean a marker tree: a tree bent to point along a trail like the Old Indian Trail-Marker Tree in Thorold. Early settlers often marked a trail by blazing trees along it, by chopping out a chunk of the bark with an axe at a level that would be easily seen by a traveller on foot or by horseback. So, some or all of these quotes may be referring to this practice.

But then I discovered this quote from the February 1880 edition of *The Canadian Methodist* magazine:

> August 10, we rose at break of day, took a little food, and started for a ride through

> the wilderness, forty miles long, no roads, and **only "blazed" or marked trees to guide us**. [Early 1800s on the Thames River west of London]

Does this mean that there were blazed trees — trees marked with an axe — *and* trees that were bent to point along trails? Maybe. The only quote I've dug up that directly talks about First Nations modifying trees is this one, from *A Journey to Canada*, by Jane Tritton Gurney (1877):

> The Indians blaze a path by cutting with an axe the barks of the large trees, and by bending the tops of smaller bushes. [Near Huntsville]

It seems plausible that some of these "smaller bushes" could also be small trees. But were the tops bent over and tied down as described by U.S. marker tree researchers, or were they just snapped to mark a temporary bearing?

A couple of other promising references from the oral history of the Haudenosaunee regarding modified trees were shared with me by Rick Hill, a Six Nations Elder and educator. Rick wrote:

> There are two references in our oral history that I'm aware of about such bent trees.

> One was a drawing made in 1779 of how warriors used to bend small saplings to help mark their trail on the war path. That has to do with warrior power. Those bent trees then grew in unusual ways serving to note the exploits of the warriors.
>
> The second was that "medicine" people would gather in the woods at night and as they collected certain medicines, they would take the branches of a tree and pull them down, then twist them together. In the morning, you could find these twisted trees, evidence that someone was there doing things that perhaps should not have been done. That is a different kind of power, associated with the power to bend trees. In either case, I'm not sure you want to follow either of those paths! Think of them as warning signs.

The drawing Rick Hill was referring to (right) is by Colonel Adam Hubley and shows modified trees in the Finger Lakes area of Upper New York State in September 1779. Colonel Hubley described two methods of how the Haudenosaunee modified trees. The following descriptions refer to the numbers on the drawing.

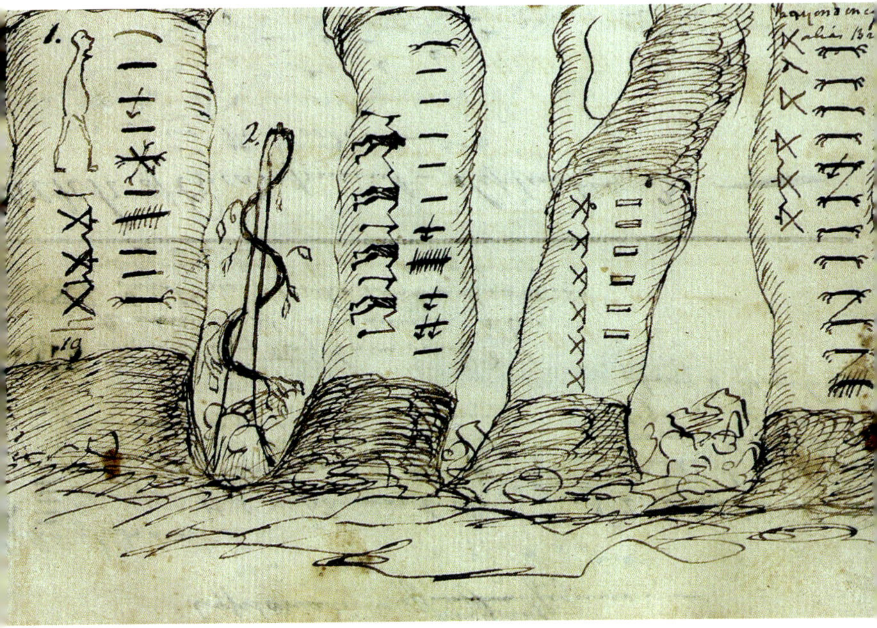

1. The Haudenosaunee stripped the trees of their bark and symbols of their war exploits were carved into them. [Refers to the four carved trunks in the drawing.]
2. A sapling was "twisted around the body, signifying they [the Haudenosaunee warriors] were strong and united." [Refers to the small twisted tree on the left hand side in the drawing.]

There is something so beautiful, sophisticated, and poetic about the notion of trail marker trees. It is incredible in this age of frenzied electronic communication to think that living, natural messages so simple and practical could be standing on the landscape today — a centuries-old tap on the shoulder pointing us along the path home. This idea reaches back to a time before the car, before roads and traffic lights, when sticking to the forest trail was crucial for survival, and a wrong turn could spell danger or even death.

It's clear that the First Nations of the lower Great Lakes did modify woody plants in some fashion or another, whether it was by bending the tops of bushes to mark a path, or by bending trees, tying them together or carving into them to send messages or warnings to others. But it's unclear whether First Nations in southern Ontario marked trees in the way that researchers in the United States describe that their Indigenous Peoples did. The Old Indian Trail-Marker Tree in Thorold was certainly bent into that shape by someone, perhaps by the Anishinaabeg (the Mississauga) who camped and hunted and lived in the Niagara area in the eighteenth and nineteenth centuries.

After inquiring with several First Nations members in southern Ontario about marker trees, the quote from the oral history of the Haudenosaunee given to me by Rick Hill was the only bit of information that was shared with me. The glaring problem is that much of the oral histories of the First Nations of southern Ontario have been lost, in large part due to the appalling racism and divisive policies of the Canadian government (and the citizens who supported those policies) over the last 150 years.

Maybe some of the trees I documented were modified by weighing them down. But maybe some of them were just naturally bent, having been trapped by a fallen tree — I've certainly seen a lot of trees like that in my travels. Maybe some of the marker trees I described started out as twitch traps set by early settlers — you know, like in the old Looney Tunes cartoons. Or perhaps some trees were bent by early wood turners to fashion furnishings for banisters or boat rails.

In our technologically driven society, we like answers. We like to point to truths with confidence. We like certainty. The acceptance of uncertainty comes easier when you study the land. By observing nature, we see that it is in flux. Nature is open and ever changing. Nature is confounding; simple, yet complex. Nature is circular: life and death, regeneration and disintegration.

So, after a lot of bushwhacking, digging through the past, and consulting with First Nations people, I've come to the conclusion that I will probably never know the truth about marker trees in southern Ontario and the Golden Horseshoe, and I'm okay with that. I'm okay with not knowing.

8

In the Stars

Sometimes I go back to Trafalgar Road hill. I'll stand on the edge like I did when I was a kid and look across the lake. I know now that it was St. Catharines and not Buffalo — not Commander Tom's home — that we saw in the distance. I look west to the McCraney and east to the Morrison and think about the adventures my friends and I had along those creeks.

I look down at the traffic lights at Iroquois Shore Road and think about The Old Trail and the First Nations who travelled on it for thousands of years.

What would it have been like to walk along the trail through the Golden Horseshoe when settlement was sparse and the land was still wild? What were the thoughts of the First Nations who walked along the trail, their hearts and minds filled with that woodsy calm? What were their thoughts about the land and The Great Woods that they walked through? Could they have imagined how the land would change?

After twenty-five years of study, my curiosity with this land and its trees continues to grow. I still explore new natural areas in the Greater Golden Horseshoe, in and around my home at the Head of the Lake, and lately, on the edges of the Golden Horseshoe in York, Durham, Northumberland, Norfolk, Brant, Oxford, and Niagara Regions.

I continue to learn new native plants; there are still many I haven't met. I'm trying to sort out those head-spinning hawthorns and stuff more grasses and sedges into my skull. I continue to seek out original trees in our streets, remnant older growth forests, and rare tree populations. I continue to work at restoring ecosystem function in our cities and towns through native plant gardening and restoration projects and

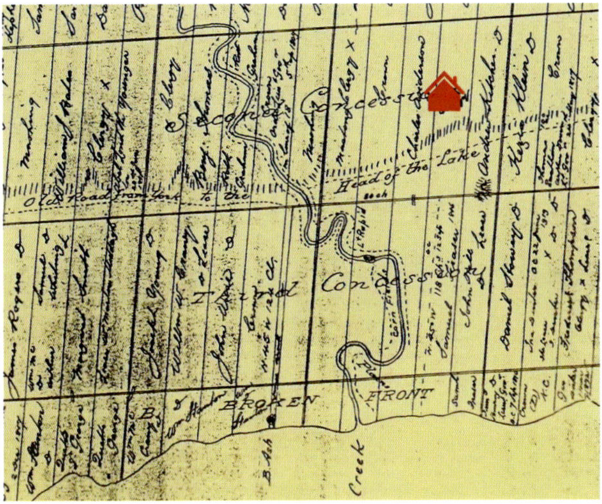

Crown Surveyor Samuel Wilmot surveyed the lands in south Halton Region in 1806 and produced this map of Trafalgar Township. The government of Upper Canada bought the lands the year before from the Mississauga First Nation. The land wouldn't become Oakville until 1827.

On the sands on the lake plain (Broken Front and 3rd Concession South), Wilmot recorded forests of pine-oak-chestnut and maple-beech-hickory-oak, with pockets of oak savannah and prairie along the lower Sixteen. On top of Trafalgar Road hill (2nd Concession South), Wilmot described forests dominated by oak, pine, hickory, and maple. On the clay plains of north Oakville (1st Concession South; cut off on the map portion shown above), Wilmot noted mixed forests of hemlock, elm, basswood, maple, beech, hickory, and oak, and swamps of speckled alder and black ash.

The dotted lines that snake along the Sixteen Mile Creek are First Nations trails that ran on the edges of the ravine. The east-west dotted line (Old Road from York to the Head of the Lake) is The Old Trail below the hill (the vertical dashes) that connected the entire Golden Horseshoe. The path has been gone for over 150 years, but I still feel its presence on the land.

invasive species control; I try to do my share in my little part of the Golden Horseshoe at the Head of the Lake.

The Greater Golden Horseshoe is a land that continues to draw me in because it's a special land. It's a land that still has original trees in its streets. It's a land of rich soils that is able to grow vibrant prairies and meadows and a wide variety of foods to sustain us. It's a land with a history of big woods and an incredible arboreal potential energy that is ready to grow new forests. It's a land of abundant fresh water and deep spiritual significance. It's a land that is a meeting place of three biomes and a gathering place for all kinds of life, including humans.

The Golden Horseshoe is a land that continues to give even when we do not. It's a land with tremendous development pressures on it and a land whose biodiversity continues to dwindle.

In *A Fair Country,* John Ralston Saul writes:

> When one Indigenous language slips away, it is as if heavy doors, once open and giving us access to a particular understanding of this place, have slammed shut, shutting us out forever. Part of our shared understanding is gone.... Each of them is a passageway into

(left) Fall colour of an old black gum in a swamp near Grassie, in Niagara Region.

> the meaning of this place. Each one lost is a
> loss of meaning and possible understanding.

Replace the word *language* with *bird*, *frog*, *turtle*, *salamander*, *snake*, *fish*, *flower*, or *tree* and the result is the same. We need to keep these doors open. With each closing door, we lose a little bit more of the understanding of and connection to our home. We lose our footing on the land.

So it is with each and every wetland that is buried, each forest lost, each original tree lost, with each Manitou that is pushed off the land. We lose the ability to understand the landscape and, therefore, the ability to understand ourselves. We lose the ability to tell ourselves stories about the land that can help shape a brighter future.

The late Henry Kock had an unusual talent for telling stories that imagined a brighter future for the Golden Horseshoe. Henry was a tireless educator on trees who worked at the University of Guelph Arboretum from 1982 to the early 2000s, first as plant propagator, and later as interpretive horticulturalist. He was a tall man with a big, bushy beard, a man who stuck out like a sore thumb riding his bicycle around campus. Henry wrote articles and taught courses on tree identification, forest education, schoolyard naturalization, and growing trees from seed. I attended as many of his talks and courses as I could, and I remember his deep and generous tone, and the inspiration and large lessons he left me with.

It was Henry who taught me about the value of the original trees in our streets, of conserving high-quality meadows and controlling invasive species. It was Henry who taught me about the importance of having at least 30 percent forest cover and harnessing the power of the trees of the field to build a "Web of Green" across southern Ontario. It was Henry who first described the Golden Horseshoe as a meeting place of three biomes. And the prominent ecologist who described the Greater Golden Horseshoe as a massive clear-cut, that was Henry, too. Henry was ahead of his time, talking about local organic agriculture, pedestrian- and bicycle-friendly streets, swimmable beaches, richly treed streets, and native plant gardens and naturalization projects at every turn.

Henry reminded us that, yes, trees are important for the reasons most people agree on: support for wildlife, shade and oxygen production, and reducing carbon dioxide levels. But he argued, "Little attention goes to the climate-moderating role of trees, by far the most significant role — so much so that all the other benefits should be understood as fringe benefits." Henry said that the whoosh of the wind in the canopy is the sound of friction, the sound of the trees slowing and lifting the wind and throwing moisture into it, thereby reducing the rate at which the earth is dried. Without tree cover, storms become more violent and localized, with higher winds and heavier rain and snow — a phenomenon we have all witnessed in recent years.

We can't all be as passionate about the land as Henry was, but if we moved closer to the natural world, we would stand more centred in our home.

Fortunately, our bodies, brains, and spirits are designed to observe the natural world. We're hardwired to experience nature. We're not hardwired to drive around in cars and sit in front of screens — hence the increasing unhappiness and anxiety that the research suggests is now at epidemic levels in the Golden Horseshoe.

We don't need to struggle so much. We need to change the way we work. We need to create more space in our lives for constructive leisure and less time for unsatisfying work. More time to follow our curiosity — more nature, more gardens, more trees, more time to consider our lives and the land around us. But to experience the gifts of the land we must start paying attention to the land. We must start building a friendship with the land. It starts with recognition. It starts with a name.

There's something connective about a name. A name is the first step to understanding, the first step to building a friendship. We must introduce ourselves and get to know the original trees in our streets. To get

In autumn, a mature red mulberry grows on a rocky escarpment slope in Hamilton Region.

to know the beech, sugar maple, white pine, hemlock, red oak, white oak, shagbark hickory, black cherry, and basswood in our forests, and the plum, sumac, white elm, trembling aspen, and bur oak in our fields. To get to know the sassafras, tuliptree, flowering dogwood, and pignut hickory on the edges, and the black ash, silver maple, white cedar, black spruce, and tamarack in our wetlands.

When you start putting names to trees, you begin to see patterns, and with those patterns comes understanding, and with understanding comes friendship, and with friendship comes respect, and with respect comes the possibility of a deeper connection — perhaps even love.

That's when the trees will start to see you coming. That's when you will begin to feel a greater connection to the land beneath your feet. Your home will become larger, your footing more sure in this great gathering place called the Golden Horseshoe.

Epilogue

A few years ago my friends and I, by then in our forties, went back to The Cool Spot. Most of the guys hadn't been back in twenty years when we set off on a magical October day of warm weather and peaking fall colours. We stopped at our old forts along the way and could still see some of the supports that we had nailed into the trees in the late 1980s. Like old times,

we built a fire on the edge of The Cool Spot, sipped beers, whittled weenie sticks, and had campfire dogs.

Sure enough, at the summit of the first climb while I was bent over examining some prairie flora, I heard the old wind at my back: "Hey Paul!? Didja find dickweed!?"

"Yes, yes, I did find dickweed," I replied, pointing back at them.

We had a great time. Post-hike emails buzzed with big thank-yous and comments like, "What a blast!" "The hike was legendary!" and "It was really fun, great memories!" We talked about organizing more hikes and making The Cool Spot Hike an annual autumn pilgrimage. We haven't done it yet.

But I know we'll gather on the edge again soon.

Because the line hasn't been broken — the friendships, the attachment to place: to the McCraney and Morrison, the Sixteen, the adventure on the edges, in the street, in the field, in the forest, on the water, and on the path. I can still follow the breadcrumbs on The Old Trail below the hill.

Acknowledgements

I'd like to thank the following individuals for their friendship, conversation, generosity, and/or companionship in the field: Donald Smith, Wasyl Bakowsky, Tony Jovan, Shawn Patille, Tom Atkinson, Nate Torenvliet, David Morris, Mark Funk, Andrew Bodrug, Steve Munday, Paul Watson, Ed Hannaford, Lyall Rudderham, Dale Hall, Sandra Ramunno, Jocelyn Perras, Kelly Breuer,

Christine Thuring, Tyrone Ramsey, Peter Ramsey, Kathy Cozens, Julia Kollek, Juby Lee, Jen Baker, Paul Smith, Tys Theysmeyer, Anne "Hummingbird" Thompson, Debbie Thain, Graham Buck, Mary Gartshore, Peter Carson, Tom Staton (thanks for the Leopold quote, dude), Albert Garofalo, Chris Davenport, Wendy Crawford, and the Newell family.

Thank you to the individuals and families who shared their unique trees, tree photos, or historical materials with me: Joyce Dunston-Reddoch, the Williams family, the Knechtel family, Mr. Jim Farr, Shirley Rothery, Whitney Lake, Jeff Beaver, Martha Howatt, Chief Reg Niganobe, Rick Hill, Terry Whalen, Susan Wells, Mark Verlinden, Brenda Bousfield, and Bill McIlveen. And to my Mississauga friends: Carolyn "Rabble-Rouser" King, Faith Rivers, Margaret Sault, Chief Stacey LaForme, Laura Jamieson, Vicki King, and Clynt King.

I'd like to extend my appreciation also to Lorraine Johnson and John Terpstra for their publishing advice and to John Ambrose, Chris Davenport, and Erin Kornfeld for reading early drafts of the book. Many thanks to Glenn Macdonald for creating the wonderful maps, to Paul Racher for reviewing the sections on First Nations history, and to Bonnie Munday at Creative Content Solutions for her fantastic editing of my manuscript before I approached a publisher. And to Dundurn Press for their great work and guidance throughout the publishing process, including Kathryn Lane, Laura Boyle, Jenny McWha, Scott Fraser, and Allison Hirst.

I would like to acknowledge naturalist George Meyers (1940–2018), who cried for the land, like all those who observe the land with their eyes and hearts wide open.

And I'd like to tip a pint to Gerry Waldron and John Ambrose for their mentorship and the wonderful botanical adventures over the years. Here's to many more.

Thanks to my family: Mom (Bernadette O'Hara), Dad (Len O'Hara), Donna, Aunt Pat, Patrick, Deirdre, Erin, Sean, and their partners and kids.

And last but not least, thanks to the old gang: Lee, Bar, Kev, Kev, Will, Stace, Graeme, Derek, Dan, Bob, James, Steve, Rick, Sean, and Cor.

Appendix 1

Native Trees of the Golden Horseshoe

#	Species	Street	Field	Forest	Water	Comments
1	Balsam Fir (*Abies balsamea*)	-	-	x	x	Native to the northern half of the Golden Horseshoe (GH). Look for the steeple-shaped crowns in cool woods and conifer swamps.
2	Manitoba Maple (*Acer negundo*)	x	x	x	x	A weedy tree of floodplains, disturbed forests, and all kinds of urban areas. Our only compound-leaved maple.
3	Black Maple (*Acer nigrum*)	x	-	x	x	A tree of forested floodplains and slopes below the Niagara Escarpment. Leaves have a characteristic wilting appearance.
4	Red Maple (*Acer rubrum*)	x	-	x	x	A versatile tree of moist to wet woods and sandy, upland forests. Brilliant red fall colour. Leaves like sugar maple, but with toothed edges.
5	Silver Maple (*Acer saccharinum*)	-	-	-	x	The characteristic tree of soft maple swamps in Southern Ontario. Commonly planted in streets and parklands.
6	Sugar Maple (*Acer saccharum*)	x	-	x	-	The most common tree in the upland forests of Southern Ontario. The tree of maple syrup. The leaf on the Canadian flag.
7	Mountain Maple (*Acer spicatum*)	-	-	x	x	A tall shrub or small tree of rocky (especially of slopes below the Niagara Escarpment) or wet woods. Uncommon in the GH.
8	Freeman's Maple (*Acer x freemanii*)	-	-	-	x	Apparently, a hybrid of red and silver maples. Not a tree that I differentiate from silver maple. They are both just soft maples to me.

#	Species	Street	Field	Forest	Water	Comments
9	Speckled Alder (*Alnus incana*)	-	-	-	x	A shrub or small tree of high-quality wetlands. Common in conifer swamps in the northern half of the GH.
10	Downy Serviceberry (*Amelanchier arborea*)	-	x	x	-	A graceful understorey tree of woodland edges and openings. Also common in hedgerows. White flowers in spring; edible berries in summer.
11	Smooth Serviceberry (*Amelanchier laevis*)	-	x	x	-	Very similar to downy serviceberry. An understorey tree of woodland edges and openings. Also common in hedgerows. White flowers in spring; edible berries in summer.
12	Pawpaw (*Asimina triloba*)	-	-	x	-	A Provincially Rare Species. A small tree found in the southern half of the GH (mostly in Niagara Region). Large, exotic-looking edible fruits.
13	Yellow Birch (*Betula alleghaniensis*)	x	-	x	x	A true forest tree of moist woods and swamps. Distinctive golden bark when young. A rare original tree, e.g., Roseland in Burlington.
14	Cherry Birch (*Betula lenta*)	-	-	x	-	An Endangered Species. The rarest native tree of the GH. Was probably more common in pre-settlement times on the lakeplain between Niagara and Hamilton before those forests were cleared.

1. List includes shrubs that can sometimes grow like trees.
2. Street trees refer only to original trees in the cities and towns of the GH, not planted trees.
3. The list of hawthorns follows Oldham, 2017.

#	Species	Street	Field	Forest	Water	Comments
15	White Birch (*Betula papyrifera*)	x	-	x	x	Also called paper birch. Iconic tree of many Group of Seven paintings. Found in swamps, woodland openings, and north- and east-facing slopes in the GH.
16	Blue-beech (*Carpinus caroliniana*)	-	-	x	x	An understorey tree of moist woods and swampy edges. Bark smooth, bluish-grey, with distinctive muscle-like ridges.
17	Bitternut Hickory (*Carya cordiformis*)	x	-	x	-	The most common hickory of upland forest habitats in the GH. Buds uniquely sulphur-yellow. Bark smooth, unlike our other native hickories.
18	Pignut Hickory (*Carya glabra*)	x	-	x	-	A Provincially Rare Species. Grows in sandy upland forest habitats with oak and white pine. A rare original tree in the streets of Brant and Niagara Regions.
19	Shellbark Hickory (*Carya laciniosa*)	-	-	x	x	A Provincially Rare Species. In the GH, found in swampy forests in Niagara Region and Norfolk County. Like shagbark hickory, but the nuts and leaves are larger.
20	Shagbark Hickory (*Carya ovata*)	x	x	x	x	A versatile tree of upland forests, swamps, hedgerows, and roadsides. Bark distinctly shaggy in appearance.
21	American Chest-nut (*Castanea dentata*)	-	-	x	-	An Endangered Species because of chestnut blight. Only a few hundred trees remain in the GH. More commonly found in the sandy woodlands of Norfolk County.
22	Hackberry (*Celtis occidentalis*)	-	-	x	x	An uncommon tree of rocky escarpment woods, bluffs, and near floodplain habitats. The edible berries are a favourite of seed-eating birds.

#	Species	Street	Field	Forest	Water	Comments
23	Dwarf Hackberry (*Celtis tenuifolia*)	-	-	x	-	Threatened. A small, scraggly tree of sandy and rocky soils. Found only in the rocky, open woods of the Niagara Gorge in the GH.
24	Buttonbush (*Cephalanthus occidentalis*)	-	-	-	x	A relatively common shrub of slough forests and thicket swamps. Usually less than two metres tall, but can sometimes grow to be a small tree up to four metres in height.
25	Pagoda Dogwood (*Cornus alternifolia*)	-	x	x	-	A common understorey tree of forest habitats, with pagoda-like branching. Sometimes found growing on rural roadsides and in hedgerows.
26	Redbud (*Cercis canadensis*)	-	-	?	-	The familiar ornamental tree with pink spring flowers. Some ecologists believe this tree may have occurred historically in Niagara Region.
27	Flowering Dogwood (*Cornus florida*)	x	-	x	-	Endangered because of dogwood anthracnose. An understorey tree of sandy, open woodlands. A rare original street tree.
28	Brainerd's Hawthorn (*Crataegus brainerdii*)	-	x	-	-	A Provincially Rare Species. Found in Hamilton and Haldimand-Norfolk Regions.
29	Pear Hawthorn (*Crataegus calpodendron*)	-	x	-	-	Vase-shaped branching pattern. Flowers in mid-June, which is late for a hawthorn. Regionally rare to uncommon in the GH.

#	Species	Street	Field	Forest	Water	Comments
30	Fireberry Hawthorn (*Crataegus chrysocarpa* var. *chrysocarpa*)	-	x	-	-	"The most northerly and cold-adapted species of hawthorn in North America" (Phipps, 2008). Named for its bright red fruits. Uncommon in the GH.
31	Scarlet Hawthorn (*Crataegus coccinea* var. *coccinea*)	-	x	-	-	Rare to uncommon in the GH. Range in Ontario nearly wholly confined to the Carolinian Zone.
32	Fuller's Hawthorn (*Crateagus coccinea* var. *fulleriana*)	-	x	-	-	A Provincially Rare Species nearly wholly confined to the Carolinian Zone. A variety of scarlet hawthorn with twenty stamen flowers and suborbicular fruits.
33	Pringle's Hawthorn (*Crataegus coccinea* var. *pringlei*)	-	x	-	-	Rare to uncommon in the GH. A variety of scarlet hawthorn with eight to ten stamen flowers and oblong fruits.
34	Kansas Hawthorn (*Crataegus coccinioides*)	-	x	-	-	A Provincially Rare Species. Confined to the Carolinian Zone of Ontario. Found only in Niagara Region in the GH.
35	White-anthered Frosted Hawthorn (*Crataegus cognata*)	-	x	-	-	An uncommon hawthorn in the GH. Flowers have white anthers.

#	Species	Street	Field	Forest	Water	Comments
36	Clustered Hawthorn (*Crataegus compacta*)	-	x	-	-	Restricted to the Carolinian Zone in Ontario. Rare in Hamilton, Brant, and Haldimand-Norfolk Regions.
37	Cockspur Hawthorn (*Crataegus crus-galli*)	-	x	-	-	A distinctive hawthorn with shiny, leathery leaves. Relatively common in the southern half of the GH.
38	Dodge's Hawthorn (*Crataegus dodgei*)	-	x	-	-	An uncommon hawthorn found at the Head of the Lake in the GH. Often has a shrubby appearance.
39	Waxy-fruited Hawthorn (*Crataegus formosa*)	-	x	-	-	A Provincially Rare Species. "One of the most beautiful hawthorns" because of its large flower size (Phipps, 2008).
40	Holmes' Hawthorn (*Crataegus holmesiana*)	-	x	-	-	A rare hawthorn that occurs throughout the GH. Similar to *C. coccinea* but with elongated fruits.
41	Copenhagen Hawthorn (*Crataegus intricata*)	-	x	-	-	A Provincially Rare Species. One extant record from Durham Region; historic records from Niagara and Haldimand-Norfolk Regions.
42	Large-thorned Hawthorn (*Crataegus macracantha*)	-	x	-	-	"The most widespread North American hawthorn" (Phipps, 2008). Can sucker to form thickets. A relatively uncommon hawthorn in the GH.

#	Species	Street	Field	Forest	Water	Comments
43	Big-fruited Hawthorn (*Crataegus macrosperma*)	-	x	-	-	One of the earliest hawthorns to flower in spring. An uncommon hawthorn that occurs throughout the GH.
44	Shining-branch Hawthorn (*Crataegus magniflora*)	-	x	-	-	A Provincially Rare Species. Found only in Hamilton Region in the GH. Leaf similar to *C. coccinea*, but larger.
45	Downy Hawthorn (*Crataegus mollis*)	-	x	-	-	Occurs only in Hamilton and Niagara Regions in the GH. Named after the noticeably hairy leaves and pedicels. One of the largest hawthorn species.
46	Pennsylvania Hawthorn (*Crataegus pennsylvanica*)	-	x	-	-	A Provincially Rare Species found in Niagara, Brant, and Haldimand-Norfolk. "Intermediate in characters between *C. mollis* and *C. coccinea* …" (Lance, 2014).
47	Poplar Hawthorn (*Crataegus populnea*)	-	x	-	-	A Provincially Rare Species found in Niagara, Hamilton, and Haldimand-Norfolk Regions. Restricted to the Carolinian Zone in Ontario.
48	Northern Hawthorn (*Crataegus pruinosa* var. *dissona*)	-	x	-	-	A Provincially Rare Species. A variety of *C. pruinosa* with ten stamen flowers (the others have twenty).
49	Small-leaved Frosted Hawthorn (*Crataegus pruinosa* var. *parvula*)	-	x	-	-	A rare hawthorn; only found in Niagara Region in the GH. Leaves small; only two to four centimetres long.

#	Species	Street	Field	Forest	Water	Comments
50	Frosted Hawthorn (*Crataegus pruinosa* var. *pruinosa*)	-	x	-	-	Rare to uncommon in the GH. Fruits often have a waxy bloom.
51	Dotted Hawthorn (*Crataegus punctata*)	-	x	x	-	One of the most common hawthorns of the GH. Grows in fields and open woodlands. Leaves have deeply impressed veins.
52	Rough Hawthorn (*Crataegus scabrida*)	-	x	-	-	A Provincially Rare Species found in Niagara, Hamilton, and Haldimand-Norfolk Regions. Varga et al. list for the GTA includes *C. scabrida* with *C. schuettei*.
53	Schuette's Hawthorn (*Crataegus schuettei*)	-	x	-	-	A rare to uncommon hawthorn in the GH. Closely resembles *C. macrosperma*.
54	Quebec Hawthorn (*Crataegus submollis*)	-	x	-	-	A rare hawthorn of the GH. Occurs only in Niagara, Toronto, York, and Durham Regions.
55	Fleshy Hawthorn (*Crataegus succulenta*)	-	x	-	-	Relatively common in the GH. Fruits bright red and succulent when ripe.
56	Eastern Burning Bush (*Euonymus atropurpureus*)	-	-	x	-	A Provincially Rare Species. A small tree or shrub of rich, high-quality forests. Can be confused with the uncommon invasive species *E. europaeus*.
57	American Beech (*Fagus grandifolia*)	x	-	x	-	A common companion of sugar maple in the upland forests of the GH. Many trees suffering from beech bark disease; trees that show resistance need to be catalogued and conserved.

#	Species	Street	Field	Forest	Water	Comments
58	White Ash (*Fraxinus americana*)	x	x	x	-	A tree of upland forests in the GH. Severe decline of trees from Emerald Ash Borer (EAB); hoping that native birds and insects will develop a taste for the non-native borer.
59	Black Ash (*Fraxinus nigra*)	-	-	x	x	A newly Threatened Species because of severe decline of trees from EAB. A common tree of swamps, with thick twigs and corky bark.
60	Red Ash (*Fraxinus pennsylvanica*)	x	x	x	x	An extremely versatile tree of fields, swamps, and early successional forests. A commonly planted street tree. Severe decline of trees from EAB.
61	Pumpkin Ash (*Fraxinus profunda*)	-	-	-	x	A Provincially Rare Species. A tree of deep deciduous swamps. Apparently, native to Niagara Region (Oldham, 2010). Also affected by EAB.
62	Honey Locust (*Gleditsia triacanthos*)	-	-	x	-	A Provincially Rare Species. Apparently native to the Niagara Gorge (Oldham, 2010) in the GH. A commonly planted street and landscape tree.
63	Kentucky Coffee Tree (*Gymnocladus dioicus*)	-	x	x	-	A Threatened Species. Apparently, native stands found in Brant, Haldimand-Norfolk, and Oxford Regions (Oldham, 2017). A commonly planted street tree.
64	Witch-hazel (*Hamamelis virginiana*)	-	-	x	-	A common, multi-stemmed shrub or small tree of upland forest environments. Look for the yellow flowers in autumn.
65	Butternut (*Juglans cinerea*)	-	-	x	-	An Endangered Species. A relatively common forest tree. Most trees in decline because of butternut canker, although some trees show resistance to the fungus.

#	Species	Street	Field	Forest	Water	Comments
66	Black Walnut (*Juglans nigra*)	x	x	x	x	A tough, relatively pest-free tree of streets, fields, floodplains, and rocky escarpment slopes. An underappreciated tree for planting and naturalizing.
67	Red Cedar (*Juniperus virginiana*)	x	x	-	-	Our native juniper. A wonderful wildlife tree and an excellent choice for planting and naturalization. One of the few native trees tolerant of salted roadsides.
68	Tamarack (*Larix laricina*)	-	-	-	x	A tree of swamps, fens, and bogs at the southern end of its range in the GH. Needles are yellow and fall off in autumn, regrowing the following spring.
69	Tuliptree (*Liriodendron tulipifera*)	x	-	x	-	Native to rich, sandy forests in the southern half of the GH. One of the tallest deciduous trees of eastern North America.
70	Cucumber Magnolia (*Magnolia acuminata*)	-	-	x	-	An Endangered Species. Native to rich, sandy forests in Niagara Region and Norfolk County; the only places in Canada where it grows.
71	Wild Crabapple (*Malus coronaria*)	-	x	-	-	Our native apple. Uncommon in fields and forest edges; mostly grows in the southern half of the GH.
72	Red Mulberry (*Morus rubra*)	-	x	x	-	An Endangered Species. Native to Hamilton and Niagara Regions in the GH. Hybridizes with the invasive white mulberry, a tree that should be culled and never planted.
73	Black Gum (*Nyssa sylvatica*)	-	-	x	x	A Provincially Rare Species. Native to the southern half of the GH, where they grow in slough forests. The oldest deciduous trees in the GH.

#	Species	Street	Field	Forest	Water	Comments
74	Ironwood (*Ostrya virginiana*)	x	-	x	-	A very common sub-canopy tree of upland forests. Some larger trees may be quite old. Also called hop-hornbeam. Member of the birch family.
75	White Spruce (*Picea glauca*)	-	-	x	x	An uncommon tree of conifer swamps in the GH. Commonly planted in conifer plantations, restoration plantings, and around residences.
76	Black Spruce (*Picea mariana*)	-	-	-	x	Uncommon in the GH. Grows in conifer swamps, fens, and around kettle lakes. Mature trees often have club-shaped tops.
77	Red Pine (*Pinus resinosa*)	-	x	x	-	A common tree in conifer plantations. Native trees are very rare in the GH. Native stands found in Halton, Peel, and Toronto Regions.
78	White Pine (*Pinus strobus*)	x	x	x	x	The Tree of Peace. The provincial tree of Ontario. A wide-ranging conifer native to fields, forests, and even on hummocks in conifer swamps.
79	Sycamore (*Platanus occidentalis*)	x	-	-	x	A rare tree of floodplains. Distinctive mottled white bark. Most street trees are the commonly planted London plane (*Platanus x acerifolia*).
80	Balsam Poplar (*Populus balsamea*)	-	-	x	x	More common in the northern half of the GH. Native to beaches, dunes, wet woods, and conifer swamps.
81	Cottonwood (*Populus deltoides*)	x	x	x	x	A common tree in floodplains, swamps, moist woods, beaches, dunes, and disturbed sites. A fast grower. Can grow to be a large tree.

#	Species	Street	Field	Forest	Water	Comments
82	Largetooth Aspen (*Populus grandidentata*)	-	x	x	-	Grows in clearings, early successional forests, forest edges, and openings on sandy soils. Like trembling aspen, but with coarsely toothed leaves.
83	Trembling Aspen (*Populus tremuloides*)	-	x	x	x	Common in fields and forest edges where it suckers through the ground to form pure stands. Grows in every province and territory in Canada.
84	American Plum (*Prunus americana*)	-	x	-	-	Grows in fields, thickets, hedgerows, and forest edges. Generally, more common in the southern half of the GH than Canada plum.
85	Canada Plum (*Prunus nigra*)	-	x	-	-	Found in fields, thickets, hedgerows, and forest edges. Generally, more common in the northern half of the GH than American plum.
86	Pin Cherry (*Prunus pensylvanica*)	-	x	x	-	Grows on rural roadsides and forest edges in the GH, often in sandy soils. Suckers through the ground to form small thickets. Distinctive dark reddish bark.
87	Black Cherry (*Prunus serotina*)	x	x	x	-	A common tree of open woods, forest edges, and thickets in the GH. Easily recognized by the dark, flaky bark, even on small trees.
88	Chokecherry (*Prunus virginiana*)	-	-	x	-	Can sometimes grow to be a small tree; often encountered as a heavily deer-browsed shrub. A common shrub in disturbed and returning forests.
89	Hoptree (*Ptelea trifoliata*)	-	-	-	x	A Species of Special Concern. A small tree native to sand dunes and river margins in Brant, Niagara, and Haldimand-Norfolk Regions in the GH.

#	Species	Street	Field	Forest	Water	Comments
90	White Oak (*Quercus alba*)	x	x	x	-	The Queen of Oaks. A tough, strong, long-lived tree of upland forests. Occurs throughout the GH.
91	Swamp White Oak (*Quercus bicolor*)	x	-	-	x	An uncommon tree of deciduous swamps on poorly drained soils. More common in the southern half of the GH. Acorns have distinctively long stalks.
92	Hill's Oak (*Quercus ellipsoidalis*)	x	x	x	-	A Provincially Rare Species of fields, hedgerows, and open woods on the Norfolk Sand Plain through Hamilton, Brant, and Haldimand-Norfolk Regions.
93	Bur Oak (*Quercus macrocarpa*)	x	x	x	x	Our toughest and most northern-growing oak. Found in fields, hedgerows, and forests, often on clay soils. A superb choice for a street or backyard tree.
94	Chinquapin Oak (*Quercus muehlenbergii*)	x	-	x	-	An uncommon oak of rocky, south-facing slopes and limestone plains in the GH. Also grows on the eastern end of Lake Ontario in the Kingston area.
95	Pin Oak (*Quercus palustris*)	x	-	-	x	A tree of swamps, slough forests, and roadsides on the Haldimand Clay Plain in Niagara Region. An excellent landscape tree for poorly drained soils.
96	Dwarf Chinquapin Oak (*Quercus prinoides*)	-	x	x	-	A Provincially Rare Species. Native to remnant prairies, sand barrens, and oak savannahs in Brant and Haldimand-Norfolk Regions in the GH.
97	Shumard Oak (*Quercus shumardii*)	-	-	x	x	A Species of Special Concern. "Distribution and status in Niagara poorly known and perhaps not present in the region at all" (Oldham, 2010).
98	Red Oak (*Quercus rubra*)	x	x	x	-	The most common oak in the upland forests of the GH. An excellent choice for planting in streets, gardens, and restoration projects.

#	Species	Street	Field	Forest	Water	Comments
99	Black Oak (*Quercus velutina*)	x	x	x	-	An uncommon oak of upland, sandy woods. The prairie and savannah oak of the GH. Mature trees have dark, often blocky-looking bark.
100	Smooth Sumac (*Rhus glabra*)	-	x	-	-	Rare in the GH. Grows in dry, sandy, open habitats. Looks like staghorn sumac but the twigs and leaf stems are hairless.
101	Staghorn Sumac (*Rhus typhina*)	x	x	-	-	A common and familiar small tree of roadsides, fields, thickets, and forest edges. Suckers through the ground to form large thickets.
102	Poison Sumac (*Rhus vernix*)	-	-	-	x	An uncommon small tree of thicket swamps and slough forest ponds. Contact with the leaves can produce a rash similar to that caused by poison ivy.
103	Peachleaf Willow (*Salix amygdaloides*)	-	-	-	x	A medium-sized tree of high-quality swamps, floodplains, and marshes. Leaves are similar to those of peach trees.
104	Bebb's Willow (*Salix bebbiana*)	-	-	-	x	A common shrub or small tree of open, wetland habitats of all kinds. Leaves wrinkled above and grey-pubescent beneath.
105	Pussy Willow (*Salix discolor*)	-	-	-	x	A common shrub or small tree of wet woods, thicket swamps, and ditches. Spring twigs with fuzzy buds are harvested for their ornamental appeal.
106	Heart-leaved Willow (*Salix eriocephala*)	-	x	-	x	A very common shrub or small tree. Grows in wet habitats of all kinds, including on sandy beaches.
107	Sandbar Willow (*Salix interior*)	-	-	-	x	As its name suggests, a common shrub or small tree of sandy or gravelly bars and creeksides. Suckers to form pure stands.

#	Species	Street	Field	Forest	Water	Comments
108	Shining Willow (*Salix lucida*)	-	-	-	x	A small, uncommon tree of high-quality wetland habitats. Trees have noticeably shiny leaves.
109	Black Willow (*Salix nigra*)	-	-	-	x	A small to medium-sized tree of high-quality swamps, floodplains, and marshes.
110	Autumn Willow (*Salix serissima*)	-	-	-	x	An uncommon shrub or small tree of high-quality wetlands. Leaves dark green and glossy above.
111	Sassafras (*Sassafras albidum*)	x	x	x	-	A medium-sized (sometimes larger) tree of sandy open woods and edges. Suckers through the ground to form many-trunked stands.
112	American Mountain-ash (*Sorbus americana*)	-	-	x	-	A small tree of central and northern Ontario. Possible record(s) for Brant County and historical records for Niagara (Oldham, 2010).
113	Northern Mountain-ash (*Sorbus decora*)	-	-	x	-	A small tree of central and northern Ontario. Rare in the GH. Two stations listed for Hamilton Region (Goodban, 2014).
114	White Cedar (*Thuja occidentalis*)	x	x	x	x	The Tree of Life. One of the four sacred medicines of some First Nations. A common landscape tree. Occurs in swamps, floodplains, on shale slopes, and rarely in upland forests. Stunted trees that grow on Niagara Escarpment cliffs are the oldest trees in the GH (see *The Last Stand*, Kelly and Larson, 2007).

#	Species	Street	Field	Forest	Water	Comments
115	Basswood (*Tilia americana*)	x	x	x	-	A common, multi-trunked tree of moist forests, roadsides, and hedgerows. A favourite tree for feeding woodpeckers and sapsuckers.
116	Hemlock (*Tsuga canadensis*)	x	-	x	-	Common conifers of shaded forest habitats, cool slopes, and swamp margins. Trees are slow-growing and very long-lived.
117	White Elm (*Ulmus americana*)	x	x	x	x	Our most common elm. Grows in a variety of habitats, in fields, thickets, swamps, and roadsides. Large trees are a rare sight because of Dutch elm disease.
118	Red Elm (*Ulmus rubra*)	-	-	x	x	An uncommon tree in the GH. Grows on rocky escarpment slopes and in floodplains. Leaves have a sandpaper-like texture. Affected by Dutch elm disease.
119	Rock Elm (*Ulmus thomasii*)	-	x	x	-	A rare and poorly understood tree in the GH. Grows on gravelly soils and limestone plains, singly and in small stands. Affected by Dutch elm disease.
120	Wild Raisin (*Viburnum nudum*)	-	-	-	x	A shrub or small tree of high-quality thicket swamps. Rare in the GH.
121	Nannyberry (*Viburnum lentago*)	-	x	-	x	A common shrub or small tree of ditches, wet fields, floodplains, and thicket swamps.

Appendix 2

Exotic Trees of the Golden Horseshoe

Species	Comments
Norway Maple (*Acer platanoides*)	An extremely aggressive invasive species in our woodlands. Should be controlled in natural areas wherever it is encountered. Should also be restricted in the nursery trade. There are so many better native tree choices.
Japanese Maple (*Acer palmatum*)	A commonly planted tree in residential gardens.
Sycamore Maple (*Acer pseudoplatanus*)	An uncommon landscape tree. An invasive species that is able to spread into native woodlands. Should not be planted.
Horse-chestnut (*Aesculus hippocastanum*)	Commonly planted on boulevards and in parklands. An uncommon invader of native woodlands.
Tree-of-heaven (*Ailanthus altissima*)	An aggressive invasive species of urban areas and adjacent native woodlands. Should be controlled wherever it is encountered.
European Alder (*Alnus glutinosa*)	An invasive species of shorelines (e.g., Cootes Paradise) and wetlands. Probably more common in the natural areas of the Golden Horseshoe than our native speckled alder.
Northern Catalpa (*Catalpa speciosa*)	A striking landscape tree with large heart-shaped leaves, showy white flowers in summer, and long bean pods in autumn (that persist into winter). Native to the eastern United States.
English Hawthorn (*Crataegus monogyna*)	An uncommon tree of fields, thickets, and forest edges.
Russian Olive (*Elaeagnus angustifolia*)	A common shrub or small tree of roadsides, especially along highways.

Species	Comments
Euonymus (*Euonymus europaeus* and *E. alatus*)	Both spindle tree (*E. europaeus*) and winged euonymus (*E. alatus*) are common landscape shrubs that sometimes spread to natural areas.
European Beech (*Fagus sylvatica*)	The commonly planted beech of older residential neighbourhoods; includes cultivars with purple leaves.
Glossy Buckthorn (*Frangula alnus*)	An extremely aggressive invasive species of moist forests, swamps, and marshy margins. Should be controlled wherever it is encountered.
European Ash (*Fraxinus excelsior*)	An uncommon landscape tree that can sometimes escape to natural areas.
Ginkgo (*Ginkgo biloba*)	A commonly planted street tree with unique-looking leaves. An over-planted street tree with no ecological value.
European Larch (*Larix decidua*)	An uncommon landscape tree. Most often seen in conifer plantations.
Common Privet (*Ligustrum vulgare*)	A common landscape shrub used for hedging. Birds spread the blue berries into thickets and forests.
Tatarian Honeysuckle (*Lonicera tatarica*)	One of a handful of non-native honeysuckles rapidly spreading into forests where they displace native shrubs and small trees. Most often a shrub about 2 metres in height, but can grow into a small tree.
Osage Orange (*Maclura pomifera*)	An uncommon small tree of rural roadsides and hedgerows with grapefruit-sized fruits. Native to the southern United States.
Saucer Magnolia (*Magnolia x soulangiana*)	The commonly planted magnolia of residential neighbourhoods, with large, showy flowers in spring.

Species	Comments
Common Apple (*Malus pumila*)	A common tree of fields, thickets, and early successional forests.
White Mulberry (*Morus alba*)	An aggressive invasive species of cities and urban woodlands. Trees should be culled, especially in Hamilton and Niagara Regions, where it hybridizes with the Endangered red mulberry.
Norway Spruce (*Picea abies*)	A common tree of residential neighbourhoods and conifer plantations.
Austrian Pine (*Pinus nigra*)	A commonly planted tree in the cities and towns of the GH.
Scots Pine (*Pinus sylvestris*)	A common tree of residential neighbourhoods and conifer plantations.
White Poplar (*Populus alba*)	Uncommon. Leaves maple-like with white undersides. Spread rapidly by suckers.
Lombardy Poplar (*Populus nigra*)	Spreads rapidly by suckers when planted on sandy sites like the Hamilton Beach Strip.
Populus x canadensis (*Populus nigra x P. deltoides*)	One of a number of hybrid poplars in the GH.
Sweet Cherry (*Prunus avium*)	A fairly common invader of thickets and disturbed forests.
Common Pear (*Pyrus communis*)	A relatively common tree of fields, thickets, and early successional forests.
English Oak (*Quercus robur*)	A fairly common landscape tree. Most often seen in fastigiate (columnar) form.

Species	Comments
Buckthorn (*Rhamnus cathartica*)	An extremely problematic invasive species. This small tree clogs the shrub layer of forests and displaces hawthorns in fields and thickets. It has been a failure of forestry departments at all levels not to have controlled this species earlier.
Black Locust (*Robinia pseudoacacia*)	Native to the eastern United States. Planted for slope stabilization and as a landscape tree in the GH.
White Willow (*Salix alba*)	Like the weeping willow, but with upright branches.
Crack Willow (*Salix euxina*)	A large willow of parklands and disturbed floodplains.
Salix x fragilis (*S. alba x S. euxina*)	The weedy willow with the reddish-orange crowns often seen in urban floodplains.
Weeping Willow *(Salix alba* var. *tristis)*	The classic "weeping willow" of gardens and parklands.
European Mountain-ash (*Sorbus aucuparia*)	An uncommon landscape tree. Sometimes escapes to natural areas.
Common Lilac (*Syringa vulgaris*)	Common on rocky escarpment soils and at old homesteads.
Little-leaf Linden (*Tilia cordata*)	A commonly planted tree in the streets of the GH.
Siberian Elm (*Ulmus pumila*)	A scourge of urban areas and highway roadsides. The MTO and urban forestry departments should be controlling this extremely invasive species.

This is not an exhaustive list of all the exotic trees that have been planted or naturalized in the Golden Horseshoe.

References

Books and Periodicals

Annual Archaeological Report. Being Part of the *Appendix to the Report to the Minister of Education Ontario*. Toronto: L.K. Cameron, 1906.

Ball, P.W. "Hill's Oak (*Quercus ellipsoidalis*) in Southern Ontario." *Canadian Field-Naturalist* 95, no. 3 (1981): 281–86.

Burghardt, Andrew F. "The Origin and Development of the Road Network of the Niagara Peninsula, Ontario, 1770–1851." *Annals of the Association of American Geographers* 59, no. 3 (1969).

References

The Canadian Biographical Dictionary and Portrait Gallery of Eminent and Self-Made Men, Ontario Volume. Toronto: American Biographical Publishing Company, 1880.

Canadian Methodist Magazine 11, no. 2 (Toronto: W. Briggs, February 1880).

Carroll, John. *Case and His Contemporaries.* Toronto: Samuel Rose, 1867.

Charlevoix, PFX. *Journal of a Voyage to North America.* London: R. and J. Dodsley, 1761.

Connon, John Robert. *Elora: The Early History of Elora, Ontario, and Vicinity.* Waterloo, ON: Wilfrid Laurier University Press, 1974.

Cunningham, Walter. *The Legend of Oromocto Spring in Attawandaron Park — Cressman's Woods.* Twenty-Fifth Annual Report, 1937. Kitchener, ON: Waterloo Historical Society, 1939, 264–66.

Day, C.M. *History of the Eastern Townships, Province of Quebec.* Montreal: J. Lovell, 1869.

Davis, Mary Byrd. *Eastern Old-Growth Forests: Prospects for Rediscovery and Recovery*. Washington, DC: Island Press, 1996.

Downes, D. *Native American Trail Marker Trees: Marking Paths Through the Wilderness.* Chicago: Chicago's Book Press, 2011.

Farrar, John Laird. *Trees in Canada*. Markham, ON: Fitzhenry & Whiteside, 1995.

Finlayson, William D., and Roger Byrne. "Investigations of Iroquoian Settlement and Subsistence Patterns at Crawford Lake, Ontario — A Preliminary Report." *Ontario Archaeology* 25 (1975).

Frank, R., and A. Anderson. *The Flora of Wellington County.* Fergus, ON: Wellington County Historical Society, 2009.

Frost, Leslie. *Forgotten Pathways of the Trent*. Don Mills, ON: Burns & MacEachern Limited, 1973.

Gannon, Dennis. "Thorold's Curious Old Tree." *St. Catharines Standard*, April 28, 2018.

Gentilcore, R. Louis, and C. Grant Head. *Ontario's History in Maps*. Toronto: University of Toronto Press, 1984.

Goldie, J. *Diary of a Journey Through Upper Canada and Some of the*

New England States. (Toronto Public Library). Privately published by Goldie's granddaughter, Theresa Goldie Falkner, 1819.

Goodban, A., W.D. Bakowsky, and B.D. Bricker. "The Historical and Present Extent and Floristic Composition of Prairie and Savanna Vegetation in the Vicinity of Hamilton, Ontario." In *Proceedings of the 15th North American Prairie Conference*, edited by C. Warwick. Grand Bend, OR: Natural Areas Association, 1999.

Goodban, A.G. "The Vascular Plants of Hamilton, Ontario." In *Hamilton Natural Areas Inventory Project*, 3rd Edition, edited by N. Schwetz, Nature Counts 2, Species List Document, 1–91. Ancaster, ON: Hamilton Conservation Authority, 2014.

Gourlay, R. *Statistical Account of Upper Canada.* East Ardsley, UK: S.R. Publishers, 1966 (orig. 1822).

Gray, Jeff. "A Defining Moment for Tkaronto." *Globe and Mail*, April 18, 2018.

Green, Rev. Anson. *The Life and Times of Rev. Anson Green.* Toronto: Methodist Book Room, 1877.

Guillet, E.C. *The Pioneer Farmer and Backwoodsman.* 2 vols. Toronto: University of Toronto Press, 1970 (orig. 1963).

———. *Pioneer Travel in Upper Canada.* Toronto: University of Toronto Press, 1933.

Gurney, J.T. "A Journey to Canada." *Cheltenham Ladies' College Magazine*, 1887.

Henderson, Bob. *Every Trail Has a Story: Heritage Travel in Canada.* Toronto: Natural Heritage Books, 2005.

Henry, M., and P. Quimby. *Ontario's Old-Growth Forests: A Guidebook Complete with History, Ecology and Maps.* Markham, ON: Fitzhenry & Whiteside, 2010.

Holden, M.R. *Burlington Bay, Beach and Heights, in History.* Hamilton, ON: William T. Lancefield, 1898.

Hosie, R.C. *Native Trees of Canada: Eighth Edition*. Don Mills, ON: Fitzhenry & Whiteside, 1979.

Hubley, A. "Adm Hubley, Jr., Lt. Colo. Comdt 11th Penna. regt: his journal, commencing at Wyoming, July 30th, 1779." Philadelphia: J.B. Lippincott, 1779 (printed 1909).

References

Jalava, J.V., M. Kanter, and S. Hodgkiss. "Be Part of the Big Picture: Big Picture Report Card Discussion Paper." Carolinian Canada Coalition, 2015.

Jameson, Anna. *Winter Studies and Summer Rambles in Canada.* London: Saunders and Otley, 1898.

Johnson, W. Stafford, and Hugh J.M. Johnston. *History of Perth County to 1967.* County of Perth, Stratford, ON, 1957.

Jones, Peter [Kakewaquonaby]. *Life and Journals of Kah-ke-wa-quo-na-by (Rev. Peter Jones), Wesleyan Missionary.* Published under the direction of the Missionary Committee, Canada Conference. Toronto: Anson Green, 1860.

Kellogg, L.P. *Early Narratives of the Northwest (1634–1699).* Vol. 19. C. Scribner's Sons, 1917.

Kernighan, R.K. "Historical Sketch of the County of Wentworth," III–XVII. In Page and Smith, *Illustrated Historical Atlas of the County of Wentworth, Ontario*. Ancaster, ON: Dundas Valley School of Art, 1971 (orig. 1875).

Kershner, B., and R.T. Leverett. *The Sierra Club Guide to the Ancient Forests of the Northeast.* San Francisco: Sierra Club Books, 2004.

King, Lloyd. *Early Days at New Credit.* Mississaugas of the New Credit First Nation, 1997.

Kock, Henry. "Growing Native Plants from Seed: Accompanying Manual to the Workshop, 10th Edition." Self-published, University of Guelph, 1998.

———. "A Life Zone Approach to Naturalization." A handout to accompany *The University of Guelph Arboretum Workshop and Interpretive Program*, March 13, 2000. Self-published, University of Guelph, 2001.

———. "Rethinking Tree Planting: A Gentle Plea for Meadows." *Green Teacher* 38 (April/May 1994).

Kock, Henry, Paul Aird, John Ambrose, and Gerry Waldron. *Growing Trees from Seed: A Practical Guide to Growing Native Trees, Vines and Shrubs*. Richmond Hill, ON: Firefly Books, 2008.

Lance, Ron. *Haws: A Guide to Hawthorns of the Southeastern United States*. Mills River, NC: Self-published, 2014.

Leopold, Aldo. *A Sand County Almanac*. New York: Oxford University Press, 1966.

Leibbrandt, Gottlieb. *Little Paradise: The Saga of the German Canadians of Waterloo County, Ontario, 1800–1975*. Kitchener, ON: Allprint, 1980.

Lewis, William H. *Aqueduct, Merrittsville and Welland: A History of the City of Welland — The Beginning Years*. Welland, ON: A.M.W. Publications, 1997.

Lizars, K.M. *The Valley of the Humber, 1615–1913*. Toronto: William Briggs, 1913.

Lytwyn, Victor. "A Dish with One Spoon: The Shared Grounds Agreement in the Great Lakes and St. Lawrence Valley Region." In *Papers of the Twenty-Eighth Algonquian Conference*, edited by David H. Pentland. Winnipeg: University of Manitoba, 1997.

Manson, Bill. *Footsteps in Time: Exploring Hamilton's Heritage Neighbourhoods*. North Shore Publishing, 2003.

Mathews, Hazel C. *Oakville and the Sixteen: The History of an Ontario Port*. Toronto: University of Toronto Press, 1953.

Maycock, Paul F., Daniel R. Gregory, and Anthony A. Reznicek. "Hill's Oak (*Quercus ellipsoidalis*) in Canada." *Canadian Field-Naturalist* 94, no. 3 (1980): 277–85.

McIlveen, W.D., and D. Bowman. "Information on a Historical Tornado in Halton." *Esquesing* 50, no. 5 (2016): 4–6.

O'Hara, Paul G. "A Call Down the Path: Trail Marker Trees in Ontario." *Field Botanists of Ontario Newsletter* 23, no. 3 (2011).

———. "Call Return: Indian Trail Marker Trees in Southern Ontario (Part Two)." *Field Botanists of Ontario Newsletter* 24, no. 3 (2012).

———. "2012/2013 Golden Horseshoe American Chestnut (*Castanea dentata*) Survey." Report submitted to the Ministry of Natural Resources — Guelph District, February 28, 2014.

Oldham, Michael J. "Checklist of the Vascular Plants of Niagara Regional Municipality." Ontario Natural Heritage Information Centre, Ministry of Natural Resources, 2010.

———. "List of the Vascular Plants of Ontario's Carolinian Zone

(Ecoregion 7E)." Peterborough, ON: Carolinian Canada and Ontario Ministry of Natural Resources and Forestry, 2017.

Oldham, M.J., and S.R. Brinker. "Rare Vascular Plants of Ontario, Fourth Edition." Peterborough, ON: Ontario Ministry of Natural Resources, 2009.

Ontario Ministry of Transportation and Communications. *Footpaths to Freeways: The Story of Ontario's Roads (Ontario's Bicentennial 1784–1984).* Toronto: Ontario Ministry of Transportation and Communications, 1984.

McLean, P., and W.D. Bakowsky. "Presettlement Vegetation Map of Halton County Based on Original Land Survey Field Notebook Notes." Unpublished. Ontario Natural Heritage Information Centre, Ministry of Natural Resources, 1999.

Pearce, Bruce M. *Historical Highlights of Norfolk County: A Volume of Norfolk History Published in 1967, Canada's Centennial of Confederation, Volume 1.* Pearce Publishing Company, 1967.

Pederson, Neil. "External Characteristics of Old Trees in the Eastern Deciduous Forest." *Natural Areas Journal* 30, no. 4 (2010): 396–407.

Phipps, James B. *Flora of North America, Vol. 9: Crataegus in eFlora.* Missouri Botanical Garden, St. Louis, MO, and Harvard University Herbaria, Cambridge, MA, 2008.

Praxis Research Associates. "Mississaugas of the New Credit Traditional Territory." Unpublished: Submitted to Margaret Sault, Research Director, Mississaugas of the New Credit First Nation, 1999.

Press, Bob. *Field Guide to the Trees of Britain and Europe.* London: New Holland, 1992.

Reznicek, A.A. "Association of Relict Prairie Flora with Indian Trails in Central Ontario," 33–39. In *Proceedings of the Eighth North American Prairie Conference,* edited by R. Brewer. Western Michigan University, Kalamazoo, 1983.

Riley, John L. *The Once and Future Great Lakes Country: An Ecological History.* Montreal, QC, and Kingston, ON: McGill-Queen's University Press, 2014.

Robinson, Dean. *The Hills of Home: North Easthope Township, 1827–1997.* North Easthope History Book Committee, 1998.

Saul, John Ralston. *A Fair Country: Telling Truths About Canada.* Toronto: Penguin, 2008.

———. *The Unconscious Civilization.* Toronto: House of Anansi Press, 1995.

Schmalz, Peter S. *The Ojibwa of Southern Ontario.* Toronto: University of Toronto Press, 1991.

Seton, E.T. *Life-Histories of Northern Animals.* New York: Charles Scribner and Sons, 1909.

Simcoe, Mrs. J.G. "*Sketch Map of Upper Canada Showing the Routes Lt. Gov. J.G. Simcoe Took on Trips Between March 1792 and September 1795.*" Map reprinted by Stonehouse Publications, St. Catharines, ON, 1795(?).

Smith, Donald B. *Sacred Feathers: The Reverend Peter Jones (Kahkewaquonaby) and the Mississauga Indians.* Toronto: University of Toronto Press, 1987.

Soper, J.H., and M. Heimberger. *Shrubs of Ontario.* Toronto: Royal Ontario Museum, 1982.

Strickland, S. *Twenty-Seven Years in Canada West.* Edmonton: M.G. Hurtig, 1853 (reprinted 1954).

Talbot, E.A. *Five Years Residence in the Canadas.* Vol. 1. Toronto: Royal Ontario Museum, 1824.

Tallamy, Doug. *Bringing Nature Home: How You Can Sustain Wildlife with Native Plants.* Portland, OR: Timber Press, 2007.

Terpstra, John. *Falling Into Place.* Kentville, NS: Gaspereau Press, 2002.

Thompson, S. *Reminiscences of a Canadian Pioneer.* Toronto: McClelland and Stewart, 1968 (orig. 1884).

Thorold and Beaverdams Historical Society. *Jubilee History of Thorold Township and Town.* Thorold, ON: Thorold Post Printing and Publishing Company, 1897–98.

Traill, Catherine Parr. *The Backwoods of Canada.* London: Charles Knight, 1836.

Turcotte, Dorothy. *Burlington: Memories of Pioneer Days.* Erin, ON: Boston Mills Press, 1989.

United States Forest Service. *Silvics of Forest Trees of the United States.* Washington, DC: U.S. Department of Agriculture, 1965.

Varga, S. et al. "Distribution and Status of the Vascular Plants of the Greater Toronto Area." Ontario Ministry of Natural Resources, Aurora District, 2000.

Voss, E.G., and A.A. Reznicek. *Field Manual of Michigan Flora.* Ann Arbor: University of Michigan Press, 2012.

Wainfleet Historical Society (Ontario). *Chronicles of Wainfleet Township: 200 Years of History.* Wainfleet Historical Society, Book Committee, 1992.

Waldron, Gerald. *Trees of the Carolinian Forest.* Erin, ON: Boston Mills Press, 2003.

Wells, Donald Raymond. *Mystery of the Trees: Native American Markers of a Cultural Way of Life that Soon May Be Gone.* Jasper, GA: Mountain Stewards Publishing, 2011.

Wentworth Historical Society. *Papers and Records of the Wentworth Historical Society.* Vol. 6. Hamilton, ON: Griffin & Richmond, 1915.

Williamson, R.F., and R.I. MacDonald. *Legacy of Stone: Ancient Life on the Niagara Frontier.* Toronto: East End Books, 1998.

Websites

1954 Aerial Photos of Southern Ontario available at University of Toronto online Map and Data Library: mdl.library.utoronto.ca/collections/air-photos/1954-air-photos-southern-ontario/index.

The Canadian County Atlas Digital Project from McGill University (2001): digital.library.mcgill.ca/countyatlas/aboutatlases.html.

Information on the history of Ontario tornados: canadatornado.com/ontario/history.

Interpreted Crown Surveyor Records by Peter Findlay (1973): uwaterloo.ca/library/geospatial/collections/digital-projects/historicalsoils-veg/index-peter-findlay.

Image Credits

Archives of Ontario: 120
Everett and Barbara Jacquith: 173 (bottom right)
The Canadian County Atlas Digital Project, McGill University: 141
Niagara Falls (Ontario) Public Library: 162
Glenn Macdonald: 11, 12, 13
Historical Society of Pennsylvania: 181
Joyce Reddoch: 173 (top right)
Library and Archives Canada: 59
Oakville Historical Society: 187
Oakville Museum: 119
Bernadette O'Hara: 72 (top)
Len O'Hara: 45
University of Toronto Online Map and Data Library: 86

All other images courtesy of Paul O'Hara.

Book Credits

Acquiring Editor: Scott Fraser
Editor: Allison Hirst
Project Editor: Jenny McWha
Proofreader: Emma Warnken Johnson

Designer: Laura Boyle